Reg Holmes

Cromwell's Ely

ELY LOCAL HISTORY PUBLICATIONS BOARD

The Board was formed late in 1973 to commission, produce and publish local history materials for sale to the general public via the book trade and to schools and education establishments via EARO. Members of the Board include members of the Ely Society, the Staff of the Ely Resource and Technology Centre and local historians. Financial support for the venture was made available by the Ely Society and EARO.

At a meeting of the Board in September 1981 the aims were rewritten — "To encourage and help people to research, write and publish papers and books on local history." With this in mind, local history materials published by anyone can carry the Ely Local History Publications Board logo provided the board has given its approval.

First published by The Ely Local History Publications Board in 1975.

Reprinted in 1982 and 2003 by The Ely Society, 23 Forehill, Ely, Cambridgeshire. CB7 4AA.

Text Copyright © Reg. Holmes 1975.
Frontispiece Illustration © Richard Ladds 1975.
Cover Design © Linda Davis 1981.

Printed by David J. Richards, 1 West Park Street, Chatteris, Cambridgeshire. PE16 6AH.

I.S.B.N. 0 903616 04 1 (Previous I.S.B.N. 0 904463 06 0)

TO

THE REVEREND CANON J.M.E. (JACK) BAGLEY

St.Mary's Church with the Sextry Barn.

CROMWELL'S ELY

FOREWORD

The student of local history who seeks to discover something of the conditions which prevailed in the City of Ely during the momentous years from 1642 to the restoration of the monarchy in 1660 will find a surprising lack of published material on the subject of his interest. The innumerable works written on the life of the Lord Protector treat of his early days, bring him to Ely at the age of 37, make some sketchy mention of the next few years of his life and pass quickly on to his progress in the realms of military and parliamentary activity. Beyond shewing the house in which Oliver lived in Ely and recounting some dubious tales of his activities in the Cathedral we can give very little enlightenment to the curious and often very much interested visitor, nor indicate where further information may be found. It seemed to me that there was scope or something to be written of the happenings in Ely at this particular period and in the following pages I have attempted to give some account of the conditions which prevailed here and how the city reacted to the upsurge of Puritan feeling which had so great an influence on the life of the community.

I would acknowledge the debt of gratitude I owe to many friends and recall the good fortune it has been mine to experience in the compilation of this work; to the Revd. Canon J.M.E. Bagley, formerly Vicar of Ely; to the Very Revd. C.P. Hankey, late Dean of Ely; to Mrs. D.M. Owen, Diocesan Archivist at Cambridge University Library; to the Governors of Parson's Charity in Ely; to the Revd. Canon D. Foulds, lately Vicar of Littleport; to Mrs. G.R. Potter of Berkeley California, U.S.A. and to Mr. G.R. Croft of Croydon. To all these I am extremely grateful and extend my sincere thanks.

I am equally conscious of the debt I owe to Derick Last, who edited my work; to Richard Ladds, who gave invaluable assistance in the lay-out and the illustrations and provided a cover for my book; to Donald Monk for his excellent photography; to Professor Willis Grant for his photograph of the Bishop's chapel and to Mrs. Jill Stockdale of Tower Farm, Little Downham for permission to use the photograph. The pen-and-ink drawing of Stuntney Manor is in the possession of Miss H.M. Thompson and she has generously given me permission to use this to illustrate my work.

REG. HOLMES.

Archery Cottage,
80 Fieldside,
Ely. Cambs.

June 1975.

THE RIGHTS OF THE COMMONERS

For the dwellers in the fenlands of Cambridgeshire, Norfolk and Lincoln the later years of the sixteenth and the early part of the seventeenth centuries brought about a revolution such as was experienced nowhere else in the country. The way of life which had been theirs from time immemorial, the isolation which they cherished and of which they boasted was in a few short years completely destroyed. In the rest of the country the clearance of forest and the extension of enclosure had been a process covering many centuries, but in spite of numerous schemes for draining the fens the district had suffered little change. The vast wastes of swamp and marsh were essentially as they had been for centuries.

However, the schemes for draining the fens which were put into operation in the early years of the seventeenth century brought about a significant change and aroused the fears of the commoners whose rights were so injuriously affected. For centuries each parish had enjoyed common rights in the surrounding fen and on these the commoners had relied for their very existence; for fishing and fowling, for the cutting of reeds with which to thatch their cottages, for the digging of turf for fuel and for summer grazing for their cattle. With the loss of their commons the fen dwellers faced ruin and starvation, and there was widespread opposition to the new undertakings.

Although the Act of 43 Elizabeth "For the recovery of manie hundred thousand acres of Marshland & other Grounds" had enjoined that the drainage "should not extend to the imparing, dymynishinge, lettinge, takinge away or extinguishinge of the intereste of the Commoners" it is quite clear that by the early years of the seventeenth century these interests were being very seriously impaired.

In 1619 the Commissioners of Sewers for the Isle of Ely petitioned the King complaining that the Undertakers "doe seeke to bring within compasse of the saide undertakinge many thousand of acres of groundes which are sometimes not drowned at all and are never so drowned but that they are worth some eight, some tenn to twentie shillinges an acre" They pointed out that "manie thousands of your Majestie's loving subjects have their chief livlyhood out of the same gounds and have lately preferred divers peticons unto us. We on their behalfe humblie beseeche your Majestie that the Undertakers may desist from medling with the groundes of that value".

Multitudes & clamours.

The petition was passed to the Privy Council, apparently pigeon-holed and conveniently forgotten. In 1630 the Undertakers were granted a Charter of Incorporation as the "Governors, Bailiffs and Commonalty of the Society of Conservators of the moors and marshes" in the counties of Cambridge, Huntingdon, Northampton, Lincoln and Norfolk.

1

Oliver Cromwell, at this time living at St. Ives, espoused the cause of the commoners and in 1636 undertook "they paying him a groat for every cow they had upon the common to hold the drainers in suit of law for five years, and that in the meantime they should enjoy every part of their common". And later, as Member of Parliament for Cambridge, he was one of those who resolved that the Commissioners "must by multitudes and clamours be withstood." It was not the drainage to which he was opposed but the injustice of the drainage awards — the allocation of large tracts of land to the undertakers and the consequent reduction of the area left for the use of the commoners.

In spite of this opposition the work of draining and embanking proceeded, and in 1638 the inhabitants of Littleport attacked the new river sluices. Loading barges with the inflammable sedge they set it on fire and allowed the vessells to drift on to the wooden sluice gates and almost completely destroyed them.

In the same year the Ely people took even more vigorous action. Under pretext of gathering for a camping game (a primitive kind of football) about a hundred of them met with the Littleport men and proceeded to tear gaps in the banks, letting the pent-up water once again flood over the fens. They were led by an Ely man who passed under the name of Edward Anderson or Powell. He was baptized at Holy Trinity in Ely 8 May 1608 Edward Powell base. His mother in 1613 was married to John Anderson, hence the alternative names applied to their son. He had been among the commoners adversely affected by the drainage undertakings and in 1636 had applied to one of the Governors of the Lands & Possessions of the Poor of Ely (Parson's Charity) for assistance. The Governor, William Cranford, sent him with a note to the Treasurer, William Marche:-

The Bearer heer of Edward Powelle is desieries to borowe XX^S of ouer monye on his cowes to help him in his ned wch Request I have grantid if the Worshipful and the rest will agre to it.
William Cranford.

William Marche consented and secured the agreement of the rest of the Governors:-

I thinke it fitting that this poore man Edward Powle should have twenty shillings out of the woorke house money lent him if he can put in securitys to pay it agayne.

William March.
John Goodericke.
Henery Goodricke.
Willm Aungier.
Willm Austen.

His bond, "in the penall sume of fforty shillings" pledges him to repay the loan at "the mansion house of John Hand situated in Elie at or uppon the ffeast of St. Luke the Evangeliste next ensuinge". It is dated 16th January 1636 and bears "the marke of Edward Powle ⅄ in the presence of Alexander Maltywarde: Torel Adam script."

Perhaps the burden of repaying the money he had borrowed proved too great for Edward Powell's resources. At any rate he appears to have been the prime mover in the desperate camping game in the fens two years later and he had no lack of support among the commoners of Ely and the surrounding district.

The disturbances lasted for several days. Nicholas Sayre, a Littleport labourer, gave evidence:- "Uppon Mondaye last I was taking up hassocks in the fenne and went from my worke to throw down a ditch in Whelpmore which the Undertakers made. I mett with Pollard Wilson and Will Howson and they asked me if I came to playe a game att footbale, and they told me Anderson would bring a ball & meet the Town of Littleport in Burnt Fen. The Lakenheath men sent worde that they would meet them & play at footbale".

John Bryce, an Ely blacksmith, said:- "On tuesday last past I went into Whelpmore to overthrow a ditch made by the Undertakers and met there with two hundred or thereabouts all of the towne of Elie, which when they met together did fflynge in part of the ditch, and we mett likewise with ffortene of ffiftene of Lakenheath men, but they did not anythinge".

The Constable of St. Mary's parish, Roman Kisby, testified against Bryce the blacksmith:- "On Wednesdaye morning last past I did see John Bryse with a camping ball and he did campe the same two furlongs into a great part of the towne, and soe Camped back agayne, and soe caried it into Whelpmore".

William Goates, a yeoman of Littleport stated that "he meeting Robert Baxter of Littleport, labourer, he the said Baxter toweld him that there was a footbale playe or campe to be holden in Whelpmore. And this informant asked him 'What, is it Saye's campe?' and he the said Baxter answered 'Noe, it will be Anderson's campe' And this informant replied 'What, doth Anderson mean to be hanged' and the saide Baxter replied that Anderson would have the first blow at the ball and would bringe with him from Elie one hundred men".

Anderson, or Powell, "to the matter of fact sayth not anythinge, but in opprobrious wordes cried out 'I will not leave my commons only I see the King's own signett & Royal assents. I will obey God and the King and noe man else, for we are all subjects. May not one be inspired and why not I to do the poor good and help them to their commons againe?"

Misdemeanours & foul speeches.

The strong Puritan convictions which were prevalent in East Anglia had led to much questioning of the spiritual authority of the Bishops, but in the Isle of Ely there was a situation which was a cause of even greater dissatisfaction. For centuries the civil jurisdiction of the Isle had been in the hands of the church. The Bishop was Chief Justice of the Isle; he appointed his own justices and magistrates, conducted criminal proceedings in his own courts and maintained his own prisons. Once his Lordship's spiritual authority had been questioned it was inevitable that doubts should be raised about the justice of allowing the civil jurisdiction to remain in his hands. Edward Powell had strong opinions on this matter, as is revealed by the "misdemeanors and foule speeches" for which he was indicted and condemned.

"When his Majesty was at Newmarket in Lent last year ye said Powell gave ye Cryer of Ely 2d and caused him to make proclamation thro ye towne that all

that would should meet ye next morne at ye Market Place to go to ye King with a
petition about their fennes." John Goodricke, one of the Justices, called Powell
before him, who said "What are ye and the rest of ye Justices? Ye are but
Bishop's Justices and not ye King's." Setting out from the Chantry, his house on
Palace Green, at five o'clock the next morning Mr. Goodricke went into the
Market Place and found there about sixty persons with cudgells in their hands
and Powell at their head. Questioned as to what he did there Powell said "I was
yesterday in your hands and heard what you would say; now you shall hear what I
have to say. I will complain of you to ye King; for ye King my master bade me tell
him of any that hinder me in my petitioning of him. Cannot you keep home and
take no notice of what we do?"

The Bishop, Matthew Wren, reported to the Privy Council "Among ye poore
people he beares and reports himself as one having ordinarie accesse & speeche
with ye King. They are told that ye King at Newmarket leand on his shoulder and
wept when he heard his relation."

Powell was committed by the Justices to the Bishop's prison, which was
then situated in the great gate of the monastery, Ely Porta. But as Sir Miles
Sandys wrote to his son at court "Word was brought to me by my Lord of
Bedford's workmen that the countrie is up against him both in Coveney and
Littleport, and I fear if present order be not taken it will turn to general rebellion in
all fenne townes." The Justices expressed to the Privy Council their fears for the

security of the prisoners at Ely, the people threatening to storm the prison and deliver Powell. Perhaps the prison in the Porta was shewing some signs of decrepitude, for later in the year the Ely carpenter, Thomas Grimmer, constructed a new door which may still be seen by the south entrance to the Cathedral; and on it he carved a set of doggerel verses:-

> 1638
> Here I was compleat in length & heigt
> The 22th of December
> Here I was set I well rember
> Tho. Grimer
> A place of care.

The verse is accompanied by a rather macabre representation of a body dangling from the gallows.

Prison Door.

5

A loathsome gaol.

By a special writ out of the Court of Chancery Powell was removed to Newgate, and from here he wrote to the Revd. William Hitch, Parson of Holy Trinity and Precentor of the Cathedral.

To his worthie and much esteemed and assured good friend Mr. Hitch, precher and deliverer of the devine misteries in the Cittie of Elie these present. Loving friends and good neighbours of the cittie of Ely and others.

You may think it strange that I am thus long deteined in prison; the truth is I might forthwith have beene delivered after the King's coming to London, had I not regarded your liberty and welfare more than my own, for the only obstacle and cause of my detention is that I will not give up your names to be fined and imprisoned as I am, altho I am continually and dayly urged thereunto, faire profers, faire offers and large promesses being annexed thereunto; that not prevailing, then threatened language, terrible speech and protestation of perpetuall imprisonment is vowed unto me. But neither there large promesses, threatenings or mine own miserie, altho greater cannot be, aswell in body as in mind, cold as yett move or shake my fidelite to you, and altho I shold endure all the miseries in the world yett wold I never be enforced thereto. May I be dealt withall accordingly by you. The truth is notwithstanding my great opposition, I can be freed if I may of twentie pounds, which underhand must be given to such as are both able and willing to procure the same, which sume I am a humble suter to you of to collect amongst you; otherwise my estate and conditon is soe lamentable and grievous as first my aged mother is in great want; my harmless children much distressed; both my wife and myself truly ruinated; beside a loathsome gaole that contains me, in which we are not only accompanied with nowsom stinkes, ould lousie lodging and all most all other miseries that can be named; so that in brefe I am amongst a laborinth of great and grievous afflictions which I cannot possible longer endure, so that I must be constrained both to publish and give up your names for the preservation of the lives of both me and mine; Charitie beginning at home if we cannot be releaved by you. But I am confident that your piety, comiseration and charitie is such that I shall not be enforced thereunto, but that you will either performe my request, which is a small matter amongst you all, or otherwise allow us a weekly maintenance and relief that we may not utterly perish until such time as it shall please God to deliver your much distressed neighbour
Edward Powell.

Good Mr. Hitch I pray you for God's cause read this first to the inhabitants of Trinitie parish, then send it to St. Maries.
To my loving friends and neighbours in the cittey of Eley thes dellver.

6

Mr. Hich,

I gladly salute you with the reste of my good friends; thees are to certifie you all in general that I am not abell to concesse anny longer but ondly for your ansre of the last lettre, for I am salesed dailly by my very good friends for the revele of their names that had a hand in the besines and then I shall have my liberty; for I will frett no longer but till the nexte retorne of the wagoner from you, soe that in shorte you will join the holle contry to gether for to condesend to my request, and I shall alwaies remain yor riall friend to command
Edward Powell.

from Newgate, London.
Nov.29 1638.
Pray be as speedy in yor ancer as posable you can, for I doe ondly stay for it.

In April Powell had been bound over to appear at the next Sessions at Ely, but the assize document bears an endorsement "Ponit loquela" (He makes an appeal) He is in Newgate". Here he remained for the next twelve months, but on May 8th 1639 the Council of the Star Chamber made an order "that he put in security before the Bishop of Ely for his good behaviour, when the Lords will give order for his discharge." On his release he returned to Ely, to his wife and two young children.

Several other Ely men were prosecuted for their part in the destruction of the river banks; the labourers Nicholas Sayre of Littleport, Andrew Sympson, Thomas Cooke and John als Pollard Wilson of Ely. With them was the Ely blacksmith John Bryse, and also Jonathan Westwood of Ely, described as "Yeoman". These were all bound over at the assizes and it would seem that only Powell as ringleader suffered imprisonment.

The Rectory of Ely.

Just two years previous to the activities of Powell and his associates Oliver Cromwell, at the age of thirty-seven had found himself called to Ely. He must have been for many years well acquainted with the problems of the area, for his mother's family had been engaged in farming in Ely for several generations. At the dissolution of the monastery in 1537 and with the establishment of King Henry's New College at Ely, Prior Welles had been appointed Dean of the Cathedral church, had relinquished his monastic name and reverted to his family name of Steward. Much of the monastic property came into the hands of succeeding members of the Steward family and at the beginning of the seventeenth century was farmed by Sir Thomas as Lord of the Manor of Stuntney. The Steward fortunes were closely parallelled by those of the Cromwells, whose landed possessions had come to them with the dissolution of Ramsey Abbey. Sir Thomas Steward and his sister Elizabeth were both born in the Stuntney manor house, which is still in existence, though unhappily in a state of dereliction.

The two families were joined by the marriage of Elizabeth to Robert Cromwell, son of Sir Henry Cromwell of Hinchinbrook, the Golden Knight, and their son Oliver was born in Huntingdon on the 25th April 1599. What is known of the first thirty years of his life is quickly told, for little evidence has survived. The family fortunes had declined since the days when his illustrious grandfather gave lavish entertainment to King Henry at Hinchinbrook, and little of what was left descended to the younger son Robert. It was as an only son among the eight children of a modest country gentleman that Oliver received his education, first at Huntingdon under the Puritan schoolmaster Thomas Beard, and later at the newly endowed Sidney Sussex College at Cambridge, which Archbishop Laud described as "a hotbed of Puritanism". In 1620, having just attained his majority, Oliver married Elizabeth Bourchier, daughter of a London fur dealer and leather dresser, who had been sufficiently successful as to acquire a knighthood; but it was as a fen farmer and possibly a brewer that Cromwell was engaged at Huntingdon for the next ten or eleven years. In 1628 he represented Huntingdon in the short-lived Parliament, which was dissolved in the following year.

In 1631 he was appointed Justice of the Peace for the borough of Huntingdon, but later in the year he sold most of his freehold property and removed to St. Ives, where he rented grazing land. He was possibly in some financial difficulty.

Five years later, in 1636, on the death of his maternal uncle Sir Thomas Steward of Stuntney, Oliver's fortunes met with a significant improvement. Sir Thomas held the Lordship of the Manor of Stuntney on lease from the Dean & Chapter of Ely and here he was engaged in sheep farming on a considerable scale. He also held the lease of the Rectory of Ely, where he farmed the tithes of the two parish churches of St. Mary and Holy Trinity.

The two parishes had from earliest times been inextricably involved in the affairs of the monastery and an appreciation of their history is offered by a glance back to the monastic days of the fourteenth century, to the time of the great Alan de Walsingham, Sacrist of the Monastery. Alan's name is famous with us for the magnificent Octagon and Lantern which he constructed in place of the Norman tower of the Cathedral which had collapsed in the year 1322, but it is not generally recognized that he systematically built up the possessions of the priory by acquiring large estates for the support of his office. The great Brayes estate which lay to the north of the Market place, and is still remembered in the modern Bray's Lane; the extensive fields of Braham farm; the entire Manor of Wentworth, all these he acquired for the augmentation of his office. For as Sacrist he was responsible for the provision of food and clothing for the brethren, in addition to the building materials which were needed for the vast work undertaken in his time.

Also appropriated to the Sacrist's office was the Rectory of Ely. The two parish churches were served by the chaplains of the Chantry on the Green, which had been founded in the year 1250 on the site of the house still known as the Chantry. The Sacrist was responsible for paying their stipends, and the revenues of the two parishes, the tithes and rents, were appropriated to his office. Adjoining the Rectory house next to St. Mary's church the Sacrist had the immense barn in which he stored the produce of the tithes which were paid to him in kind.

Oliver's inheritance.

Such was the situation until the monastery was suppressed in 1539 and the prior and brethren emerged as the Dean & Chapter. The Rectory was farmed out under a lease to a lay Rector, who paid a stipulated sum to the Dean & Chapter and then collected for his own use the tithes and rents due from the properties in Ely.

This was the lease which was held by Sir Thomas Steward at the time of his death in 1636 and which he bequeathed to his nephew Oliver Cromwell.

"The Rectory & Parsonage of ye Holy Trinity and St. Mary ye Virgin of Ely called or known by the name of the Sextry in Ely, and also the Chappell of Chetisham, with their rights, Members & appurtenances is impropriate and belonging to the Dean & Chapter of Ely.

It consisteth of a fair Parsonage house built with Brick and Stone, and covered with Tyles, containing a Hall, a Parlor, a Kitchen, Buttery, Larder, Milkhouse and other necessary Roomes with Chambers over them. A Fair Parsonage Barn called ye Sextry Barn standing within the yard, with other necessary out houses & Lodges pertaining to the Barn called ye Grange. And also of one close of pasture in Bugg's Lane, called Mill Close about Two acres, and Fourscore and Tenn acres of arrable & laies in the Fields called Breewood and in the other fields of Ely.

And also of all manner of Tythes of Corn & Hay and all other Tythes, oblacions, profitts, Commodities and emoluments to ye said Rectory belonging; and also of all ye Tythes &c belonging to ye Chappell of Chetisham, all which is situate in Ely and Chetisham in the Isle of Ely & County of Cambridge."

The Lessee was required to pay to the Dean & Chapter a total of £68 per annum and "five Quarters of the best white wheat at Christmas and Lady Day; one Boar yearly on St. Luke's day or 40 shillings in money; and five Cart Loads of Wheat Straw and five Cart Loads of Barley Strawe yearly by equall portions to be delivered at the Stables within the precincts of the College upon All Saints Day, upon the Nativity of Our Lord and the purification of the virgin, called Candlemas Day."

He also had to pay "the Sallary of Tenn pounds apeece to two Chaplains which he should appoint to celebrate divine Service and attend ye Cure in the parochial Churches of ye Holy Trinity and St. Maries in the Town of Ely." He covenanted "to maintain and re-edifie the Chancell of the Church of St. Maries in Ely and all the Walls, Edifices, buildings & Hedges and other reparacions to the said Rectory belonging, and at the end of the Term repaired & fenced to leave them."

The tithes which the farmer received were very substantial; one of every ten sheaves of wheat or barley; the tenth bale of hay; a similar proportion of the piglets and calves, chickens, ducks and geese and of eggs. The Sextry barn was of immense proportions; when it was demolished in 1842 in the face of vigorous protests from antiquarians throughout the country it was claimed to be the largest barn in England — 40 feet wide, 232 in length and 69 feet high. It covered much of the ground now occupied by the Parson's Charity almshouses adjoining the vicarage, and nothing of the building now remains but part of a thirteenth century double-lancet window which is built into the wall of the vicarage garage.

The Rectory house was enlarged at this period, possibly during the time of Oliver's occupation. Part of the courtyard at the rear of the building, overlooked by a timber gallery on the first floor, was roofed in and a new chamber built on the west side. From the window of this chamber, now known as the Cromwell room, the farmer or his servant could look down on the carts laden with the produce which was brought into the yard for storage in the great barn.

Thirteenth Century Window.

The profits and emoluments which accrued to Cromwell as a result of his uncle's bequest were substantial. When under the Commonwealth a few years later the Parliamentary Commissioners made a valuation of the Rectory they declared it to be worth £344.6.8d per annum, an amount of money which at seventeenth century values would place the recipient in the higher income range. Oliver also acquired other land in Ely, which he leased from Clare College in Cambridge. One piece of land, later known as Swain's Close, lay at the north end of Lisle Lane and had been in the possession of Sir Thomas Steward, lying next to "the holt called the Bell holt of the North part" and "abutting upon the north next unto a parcell of ground sometime the vineyard of the Lord Bishop of Ely Three score and tenn yards".

Cromwell 1656. By Mike Young

from Cooper's Drawing of a miniature.

Another of the Clare College possessions was leased from "the feast of St. Michael 1636" by an indenture between "Thomas Paske D.D., Keeper of Clare, and Oliver Cromwell of the Cittie of Elie, Esquire. "One piece or plott of ground sett, lying and being in Newnham within the said Cittie of Elie conteyning in length fortie yardes even soe as it lyethe betwene the lands of the Almoner of the Abbie of Elie East and West abutting upon the King's highway South; and against the Close of the Prior of Elie called Parradise on the North." The indenture bears Cromwell's signature.

In the tempestuous years which were to follow Oliver and Madam Cromwell must often have looked back with longing to the quiet peaceful days they spent in the Rectory house at Ely. Andrew Marvell wrote of Cromwell as he looked out on the world from his calm seclusion:-

> "From his private gardens, where
> He lived reservéd and austere
> As if his highest plot
> To plant the bergamot."

The bergamot still grows in the vicarage garden by St. Mary's church.

Care of the poor.

Oliver quickly became involved in the affairs of the city. His uncle had been Treasurer and one of the foremost of the Feoffees of Parson's Charity, which had been established in Ely in the fifteenth century. A memorandum in the charity minute book records that on the 30th August 1636 the Feoffees "did meete at one Mr. Micah Wickham his house in the Cittie of Ely and then and there with one consent did Elect and Chuse the Right Reverend ffather in God ffrancis, Lord Bishop of Ely, William ffuler, Doctor of Divinity and Deane of Ely, Oliver Cromwell Esqr., Antony Page of Ely, Gent. and William Austen of Ely, yeoman, to bee ffeoffees of Lands of the poore of Ely according to the King's letters Patents granted & dated in the nynth yeare of his Reigne 6° January Anno Dni 1633".

The house of Micah Wickham, no doubt an inn, was situated in what was then the important waterside district at the foot of Fore Hill. When a few years later it passed into the hands of the Goodricke family it was known as "The Crown" and later became the "Three Crowns" with its attractive double gable and blacksmith's shop. It retained its licence well into the present century and the corner on which it stands is still known as "Crown Point".

During the next few years Cromwell was active in the charity affairs which provided relief for the sick and poor of the city. In the "Memoirs of the Protector Oliver Cromwell" published in 1820 by Oliver Cromwell Esqr. the transcript of a letter written to the Treasurer of the Charity is printed.

The old Three Crowns

Photo Donald Monk

Mr. Hand,

I doubt not but I shall be as good as my word for your monie. I desier you to deliver 40s of the town monie to this bearer, to pay for the phisicke for Benson's cure. If the gentlemen will not allow it at the tyme of accounts, keep this noat, and I will pay it out of my own purse.

Soe I rest
Your lovinge friend
Sept 13 1638   Oliver Cromwell.

For some years relief had been afforded to William Benson. The charity accounts for 1636 contain an item "for phisicke & surgery to old Benson £2.7.4d", and in the next year "To Benson at divers times 15s.0d." There is however nothing in the accounts for 1638 to shew that any payment was made to this man by the feoffees in that year; it would seem that Oliver was called upon to provide the 40s from his own purse.

The account book of the charity provides further evidence of Cromwell's activities. Just prior to his death Sir Thomas Steward had received the sum of ten pounds from "Mr. Noye, the King's Attorney Generall, to be imployed to buy Cowes for the benefitt of the poore of Ely". William Noye had gained great notoriety on account of the measures he employed to raise money for King Charles, and two years before Cromwell's appearance in Ely he had introduced the démand for the payment of Ship Money, which was to prove thoroughly obnoxious throughout the country. It is ironical that his gift to Ely should have come into the hands of one of his most vociferous critics, for the charity account book has an entry in Cromwell's handwriting:-

"This tenn pounds was payed by Mr. Archdeacon Wigmore upon the first of ffebruarie into the hands of John Hand in the presence of us

Oliver Cromwell.   HE Goodericke.
John Hand.   Willyam Cranford."

Several bonds secured in the year 1638 mention Cromwell as a Governor of the Charity, but no other documents bearing his signature have survived.

Arch-enemy of the Puritans.

In 1638, two years after Cromwell's arrival in Ely, Matthew Wren was translated to the Bishopric of the Diocese. He was a churchman of the school of Archbishop Laud and was strongly opposed to the Puritan cause. He had been appointed to the Bishopric of Norwich in 1635 specifically to counteract the spread of Puritanism in East Anglia and his efforts to restore to that diocese the High Church practices of the Archbishop had brought him into great disfavour in many of the parishes where Puritanism was strongly entrenched. His translation to Ely was no doubt made with the intention of curbing the growing power of the Puritans in the University of Cambridge.

Wren's fervent desire to restore to the church the dignity and ceremonial which was anathema to many of his flock brought about a state of conflict which was not lessened by his cantankerous and headstrong nature. He was regarded as second only to Archbishop Laud as the arch-enemy of the Puritan cause. He was a supporter, and indeed named as the chief instigator, of the disastrous Bishops' War which in 1639 sought to impose on the Scottish Presbyterians the Laudian Prayer Book. He certainly raised troops and arms for the war.

On the 17th April 1639 the Dean & Chapter "Delivered to Mr. Dr. Brown the sume of £72 for the Churche towards His Majesties Warrs." And among the documents in Littleport parish chest is one dated the first of April in the same year:-

Recvd this day of the Constable of Littleport the sum of 12¹ 10s towards the Colling, Conducting & Transporting of soldiers out of this County of Cambridge for his Majesties service. Luckwise I recvd before this time the sume of 59s 3d Towards the furnishing of the store house for this County of pouder & bullets & match which was due for the town of Littellporte. Recvd more of the foresayd Cunstabells the sume of 4s 2d for the muster masters fee.

John Cole

John Cole is revealed to be Chief Constable and a resident of Little Downham, where he lived in close proximity to the magnificent palace which Bishop Wren occupied in that place.

In 1640 Cromwell was returned to Parliament as a member for Cambridge. His first speech in the Long Parliament was in support of nine articles of impeachment drawn up against Bishop Wren and he served on the Parliamentary committee appointed to deal with the matter. Wren was voted unfit to hold office in Church or State.

Matthew Wren Bishop of Ely.

Wakes & feasts.

In the same year a petition signed by some hundreds of Cambridgeshire men from the southern part of the county was presented to Parliament. A list of thirteen articles of complaint contains protestations against "the Bishop's own personal example in bowling, wakes and feastes, with beastlie drunkenness, lascivious dauncings, quarrellings & fightings, which more suit with dedicacions of Temples to Bacchus & Venus then to the service of Almighty God."

A sixteenth century writer Philip Stubs, in his "Anatomie of Abuses" gives an account of the so-called Church Ales which the Puritans were horrified to find Bishop Wren was seeking to restore to their churches. In 1595 Stubs had written:-

"In certaine townes where drunken Bacchus bears sway against Christmas & Easter, Whitsunday or some other time the churchwardens of every parish with the consent of the whole parish provide half a score or twentie quarters of mault, whereof some they buy of the church stocke & some is given to them of the parishioners themselves, everyone conferring somewhat accordinge to his ability. Which mault being made into very strong ale or beer is set to sale either in the church or in some other place assigned to that purpose. Then when this nippitatum, this huffe cappe, as they call it, is set abroach, well is he that can get the soonest to it, and spends the most at it; for he is counted the godliest man of all the rest and most in God's favour, because it is spent upon his church forsooth. They bestow that money that is got thereby for the repaire of their churches & chappels; they buy bookes for the service, cupps for the celebration of the Sacrament, surplesses for Sir John, and such other necessaries."

There is no doubt that the brewing of Church Ales had been practiced in Ely. An item in the accounts of St. Mary's church shews that £9 of the parish stock in the year 1578 "is converted into forty coomes of maulte, which maulte do remayn in Robert Silvertop's to the use of the parish." Robert Silvertop's maltings lay just over the church-yard wall, on the site in Church Lane later to be occupied by the public house "The Malt & Hops".

The Bishop had allowed and encouraged the holding of livings in plurality. "Incumbents seldom preach, but secure anie ignorant minister such as they may hire. Many vicarages are Rectories belonging to the bishop, the Dean & Chapter and the Colleges; many are under £20 per annum, and sufficient ministers will not accept them."

The criticism ranged over a variety of subjects; "The infinite number of matters daily presented in spiritual courts and intolerable illegal fees exacted." The Bishop had issued an interdict "on religious discussion in private houses, at Trencher meetings and amidst their cupps to dispute on articles of religion." He had caused to be set up "Tables altarwise, rails and steps, at the expense of the parrishes." He had introduced into the churches "Pictures of the Trinitie and B.V.M."

"Many expect revolt of our church by reason of the late popish innovations by the Bishop." "Divers farmers have left the country and sold their lands & stock with great losse, to seek peace and comfort they could not enjoy with us."

When in 1641 the Bishops were excluded from the House of Lords Wren joined with others of their number in a protest against all proceedings of the House during their expulsion. They were charged with High Treason and on the 30th December committed to the Tower. Wren remained in prison for some months, but was released on the 6th May in the following year and retired to his palace at Little Downham. Since Bishop Goodriche's days the palace on the green at Ely had been allowed to fall into decay and was uninhabitable.

Cromwell, or at least members of his family, was still living in Ely. He paid to the Bishop for the property he was holding of the Manor of Ely Barton his rent for the Christmas quarter 1641. He was evidently still carrying on the fight for the rights of the commoners in the fens. Clause 32 of the Grand Remonstrance presented to the King on the first of December 1641 protested that "Large quantities of common land and several grounds hath been taken from the subject by colour of the Statute of Improvement and by abuse of the Commission of Sewers without their consent and against it."

Wrangling reckonings.

Many of the Ministers of the churches in the Ely diocese had great sympathy with the Puritan cause, but amongst those of the opposite faction was John Hill, Minister of Coveney with Maney. He was a high-churchman who aroused feelings of great resentment amongst his parishioners. They drew up a long list of his misdemeanours. "He hath preached but once by the space of a year at their chappell at Maney, and when he did soe come they were constrayned both to fetch him & carry him backe again, & payed for his diett at their own charges, bothe for himselfe and his fellowes. He hath neither given them sermon upon the Sabbath day these twenty yeares, although they have paid him his full dues and tythes."

When he administered the Sacrament to them it was his usual course "to have wrangling reckonings, to the great disturbance of the mindes of the communicants in soe holy a service; there are belonging to the Chappell of Maney about 100 communicants and he forceth them to find a Curate at their owne charge."

One of his parishioners, Edward Holmes, deposed that his mother had died and he had caused her to be carried to Coveney to be buried there according to custom "with many of his neighbours attending her buriall; and when they came to the grave, no minister could be found to bury the corpse. Whereupon they were forced to leave the said corpse at the grave unburied, and he cannot tell when or in what manner she was afterwards buried".

Katharine Holmes, a widow, had been sued by Dr. Hill "for a Tythe Calfe, and he caused her to give him foure Nobles for composition with him; wherewith he bought a Communion table and sett it in the Chancell, with these wordes engraven upon it "Take heed, sin noe more, lest a worse thing come unto thee." All affirmed that Dr. Hill had shewn great disaffection towards Parliament.

However, not all of the witnesses were inimical to the Doctor; four of his Coveney parishioners testified that his usual custom "is to preach once a month with them and sometimes twice." If Dr. Hill felt the necessity for defending his apparent neglect of his Manea parishioners he could have called attention to the fact that the recent construction of the Bedford Level channel had effectively separated his two churches; whereas the distance by road between Coveney and Manea had been about five miles the Old Bedford now lay between the two villages and it had become necessary for any approach by road to be made by way of Earith — a journey of some eighteen miles.

The King's Proclamation.

With the impeachment and execution of the Earl of Strafford and the imprisonment of Archbishop Laud the conflict between the King and Parliament was brought to a head. The inevitable resort to arms came and Robert Devereux, Earl of Essex, began to raise troops to promote the cause of Parliament against those of the Royalist faction. The King reacted immediately by issuing a proclamation declaring Essex a traitor, and ordered this to be read publicly throughout the country.

The Dolphin Inn.

Parliamentary Major Dodson was enjoying a quiet drink in the Dolphin Inn on the Market Place at Ely when he was disturbed by the noise of the Bishop's crier announcing the King's proclamation which he was about to read. The major rushed out and accosted the crier, demanding "who sett him at work; the cryer made answer, what have you to do withall. Whereupon Major Dodson saide whoever read it, he would have his hand cutt off. Whereupon there had likely to have been a Muteny, there being a great concourse of people, amongst whome was Mr. Hill, the parson of Coveney, together with Mr. Andrewes a Councillor, and Mr. Holman, Deputy Bayliffe, great sticklers to have the proclamation made openly in the face of the country." Dr. Hill straightway entered the Shire Hall on the Market Place, where the Assizes were being held, "and charged men with halberds to assist him that published the proclamation." Captain Humberstone March, himself a Parliamentary sympathiser, and Mr. Barries, another of the Justices, advised Major Dodson to "gett out of Towne, for that there were some about to draw up articles against him and that thereby he might receive some damage wherein they could not help him, the Bishop and his friends being soe powerfull".

The attorney, Torrell Adam, gave evidence that Dr. Hill "did desire him to draw up articles against Major Dodson for opposing him about the proclamation". Torrell Adam was one of the Cathedral Lay Clerks; he had been a choir-boy and his name is to be found with those of many other boys carved on the wall of Bishop Alcock's chapel in the Cathedral.

Doctor Hill received a short term of imprisonment for his part in the affair on the market place, and it is evident that his disaffected parishioners were anxious to be rid of him. Three of his flock deposed that "the next day after he had his liberty out of prison in Cambridge they did see him soe drunke at Ely that he could hardly sit upon his horse back, reeling first to the one side, then to the other." Eventually he appears to have been ejected from his living as one of the Scandalous Ministers so obnoxious to the Puritan churchmen.

However, one Ely man had cause to be grateful to Dr. Hill. It was Edward Powell, the man who in 1638 had been incarcerated in Newgate for his part in the fen riots. Dr. Hill had stood surety for him and had been bound in the sum of ten pounds to secure his appearance at the Ely Assizes.

Lands & Possessions of the Poor.

We have seen that almost immediately upon his coming to Ely Cromwell had been closely involved in the affairs of the city and had been appointed one of the feoffees of the old-established charity founded by Thomas Parson in the fifteenth century. Thomas Parson had bequeathed to the town certain properties in the neighbourhood and had stipulated that the revenues should be employed for the payment of the tenths and fifteenths which from time to time were levied on the citizens for the personal use of the reigning monarch. The fifteenths were frequently granted by Parliament to Queen Elizabeth and continued on behalf of James I, though they were less frequently made in his time. In the succeeding reign, from the time when Charles dismissed his parliament in 1629, none at all were levied on his behalf. Consequently the money arising from the rents and revenues "did lie dead in the hands of the feoffees" and in 1633 a charter was obtained ordaining "that there should be one body corporate and politic consisting of the bishop, dean and archdeacon for the time being and nine other persons residing in the city, who should be called by the name of the Governors of the Lands & Possessions of the Poor of Ely." To this Corporation all the possessions, the powers and responsibilities of the feoffees of Parson's Charity were conveyed, and gradually the Governors took over the responsibility for relief of the poor and established their own workhouse in the town. It was to this body that Oliver Cromwell was elected in 1638, as we have already noted, but it is clear that the Corporation was from the first dominated by the high ecclesiastical dignitaries who were proving unacceptable to the very substantial Puritan element in Ely.

On the first of June 1641 two of the parishioners of Holy Trinity, Thomas Fowler of Chetisham and Thomas Canton of Ely, put forward on behalf of the citizens two petitions to the House of Lords. In the first of these they alleged that there had been misuse of the Parson's Charity funds; that the rents received by the Governors "have not beene in any considerable measure imployed for the benefitt of ye Inhabitants for 16 yeares past. Ye whole benefitt is withholden (by the Governors) to their proper and particular behoofe, for remedy in which your Petitioners are not able to seeke reliefe against ye said ffeoffees, being persons of great purse & eminent quality." They prayed that the Lords should call for the charters and evidences which were being held by the Governors and should cause an account to be made of the money they had received over the previous sixteen years.

The House of Lords dealt with the petition with what must be recognized as exemplary promptitude, for on the following day, the second of June, they made an order "That the Petitions of Thomas Fowler, Thomas Canton and others on the Behalf of the Inhabitants of the City of Elye are referred to the Committee for Petitions to consider them." It may be remarked that the Ely petition was one of the first of a very great number made to the Lords at this time. Their journals record that in August of that year so many were being submitted that an order was made "that no more petitions be received by this house".

The Ely petitioners drew up a list of the noble lords serving on the Committee for Petitions, a list of fifty-one names, which incidentally included the seven bishops of Durham, Winchester, Lincoln, Exeter, Ely, Rochester and Chichester. "Mr. Justice Heath and Mr. Justice Reeves" were to attend their Lordships, "and such others of the King's learned Councell as their Lordships shall please to call. Their Lordships, or any of them, are to meete every Tuesday and Thursday at 2 of the Clocke in the afternoone in the Privy Chamber."

A month later, on the sixth of July, the Ely inhabitants received a notice signed by "Jo. Browne, Clerk to the Parliament", the man who was responsible for drafting the Grand Remonstrance.

Die martis sexto die Julij 1641.
The petition of Thomas ffowler and Thomas Canton on the behalfe of themselves and other the Inhabitants of the Citty of Ely beinge read before the Right Honble the Lords Comittees for peticons in the High Court of parliamt their Lordshipps doe recommend the peticoners cause and matters in theire peticon sett forth to the Right Honble the Lord Keeper of the Greate Seale of England, that hee doe expedite the cause with equity accordinge to the Justice thereof.
Jo: Browne.
Cleric. Parliamentore.

It was not until the following January, however, that a commission was set up "out of his Majesties high Court of Chauncery, directed to us his Majesties Commissioners Thomas Duckett, Thomas Symonds and Dudley Pope, Esquiers..... att the Inn called the Dolphin touching certaine Lands & moneyes given by one Thomas Person & others to the charitable use of the Inhabitants of the saide Cittie for the space of sixteen yeares last past". It may be remarked that in the Charity account book the words "his Majesties Commissioners" have been struck through with a pen, no doubt by some fervent supporter of the Royalist cause who refused to accept the legality of the proceedings.

The "Accompte" was taken on the 25th January 1641/2 and the evidence given by some of the witnesses who were called would suggest that the Ely people certainly had reason for questioning the way in which affairs had been conducted. Anthony Page said "that hee hath heard that his name hath beene used as a nominated ffeoffee; but hee doth not know by what Authority hee was thereunto chosen or ever was called into any of the said meeteings, nor did consent unto the disposinge of any the said Revenues of the said Lands." William Austen averred "that hee hath beene called by some of his Neighbours a feoffee for the lands late Persons, but whether hee bee indeed a feoffee, yea or nay hee knoweth not."

"William March, Esquier, beeing one of the feoffees, saith that for these sixteene yeares last past hee was never called to any of the Accompts or reckoninges amongst the rest of the ffeoffees. Neither did hee know of their Charter till after they had procured it." He had ten pounds of the feoffees money, five of which he repaid and the other five was spent "when the controversie was betweene Cambridgesheire and the Isleland concerning Shipp money, which five pounds the Country have agreed to paye back." Since Sir Thomas Steward's time, he claimed, the Archdeacon, Daniel Wigmore "had the whole dealeing and manageing of the busienes."

The Archdeacon appears to have been the prime mover in the scheme for "setting the poor on worke" in a spinning house which had been established in the city. Wool from Sir Thomas Steward's sheep at Stuntney and Barton Farm in Ely, and also that from the farm of Henry Gooderick at New Barnes, was spun into thread and taken by pack-horse for sale in Norwich and Cambridge, and for a time the trade prospered, both in the workhouse and in private houses, for the spinners "drawed out their work soe fine" that it could be sold for a much better price than formerly. The venture, however, suffered a severe setback in the year when the plague visited Ely "and the worke brake up." No accounts appear to have been kept and the affairs of the charity were so involved that it was necessary for the Commissioners to call a further meeting on the 2nd March at Cambridge, where they met "att the Inn called the halfe Moone." Here accounts were produced covering some three thousand pounds, but a further £700 was never accounted for.

The two feoffees John Hand and William Cranford, who had been responsible for collecting the rents of the charity properties, claimed that "they had never disposed of any part therof but by the direction & appointment of Mr. Daniel Wigmore, Mr. William Marsh and Mr. Oliver Cromwell."

No sermons in church.

At the same time as they submitted to the House of Lords their petition regarding Parson's Charity the two Ely men, Thomas Fowler and Thomas Canton, put forward a second petition. This called for a reformation of the church services in Ely and was directed specifically against the Dean & Chapter of the Cathedral, who were impropriators of the tythes of the two parishes of Holy Trinity and St. Mary's.

To the right honble the Lords in the high Court of Parliament Assembled:

The humble Peticon of Thomas ffowler and Thomas Canton on the behalfe of themselves and of ye rest ye Inhabitants of the Citty of Ely:

Sheweth:

That in ye said Citty & precincts thereof & hamletts thereto belonging there are about 1300 ffamilyes, 2 Parish Churches and 2 Chappells of ease, all unendowed & ye Cures served by Stypendaryes; that is to say ye 2 Parish Churches by 2 of ye quire for 10^{li} a peece & ye Chappells of ease by 2 Curates for 1^l 6s 8d a peece Salary. That ye Deane & Chapter of Ely are ye impropriators of ye Sextary in Ely to which belongeth all sorts of tythes and offerings wch are worth yearely at least 600^{li} and ought to repaire ye church of ye Trinity in Ely comonly called St. Maryes Chappel.

That such who doe officiate ye Cure in ye said Parish Churches are able and honest men, willing to take paynes and worthy of better provision, but ye said Deane & Chapter doe confine ye Sermons to ye Cathedrall & enioyne your Petitioners to repayre thither, and that alsoe but once every Lords day, there being noe sermon att their proper Parish Churches, soe much as on those dayes when ye Sacrament is administered.

That ye howers of prayer in ye morning are unseasonably early, soe that aged people, servants and Children can not with any convenience repayre to Church espetially in Winter tyme, and moreover by reason of almost an howers distance betweene ye service ended in the said Churches and Sermon begun in the Cathedrall itt often happeneth that Servants withdrawe themselves from Church and they and sometimes Masters of ffamilyes alsoe fall into Alehowses and Tavernes to the dishonour of God in breach of the Sabbath and defaceing his Image by drunkeness, and the said Chapter doth suffer the said Church and Chappell to fall to great decaye.

That divers of ye Prebends doe lett their lodgings to Persons of greate estate, who in countenance of their residence there doe exempt themselves from the dutyes to ye Towne to which all other Townesmen are contributory.

ffor remedy in all whch your Petitioners humbly praye that ye said Deane & Chapter may out of the said Sextary or othrwise give a sufficient allowance to 2 able ministers who maye fully intend the Cures of ye said 2 Churches and that your Petitioners maye have sermons there and not bee tyed to attend in ye Cathedrall, and that ye said Chapter maye make allso provision in some fitting measure for supplye of ye said Chappells with sufficient Curates and mayntenance for them and that they may bee compelled to repayre ye said Church and Chappell to prevent a Charge to fall upon your Petitioners. And that theire tenants to their severall lodgings may bee rendered lyable to ye payement of like dutyes with others the inhabitants.

And they shall ever pray for the happie issue of this great Councell.

Thomas ffowler.

Thomas   Canton.

1 Jany. 1641.   ⵉⵉ   *marke*
                                      of

As with the petition for an examination of the Charity affairs that concerning the church services received immediate attention by the House of Lords. On the 6th July 1641 the Clerk to the Parliaments informed the Ely petitioners "It is this day ordered by their Lordshipps that the Deane & Chapter of Ely may have a coppy of the petition and that they shall within tenn days after notice hereof make an answer thereunto in wrightinge and present the same to theire Lordshipps, and then theire Lordshipps will take such further course therein as shallbee agreable with justice and equity."

The answer of the Dean & Prebends.
The answer of the Dean & Chapter, signed by Dean Fuller and two of the Prebendaries, was submitted to the Lords.

To the right honorable the Lords assembled in Parliament.
The humble Answere of the Deane and Prebends of the Cathedrall Church of Ely to a peticon Exhibited in the names of the inhabitants of the Cittie of Ely.
Shewinge
That the inhabitants of Ely have uppon the Sabbath day in the forenoone usuallie repayred to the Cathedrall Church to Sermon. The Dean and Prebends Each Sabbath day constantly preachinge in that Church, which Course was the Rather observed for that one of the two parish Churches in the said Cittie was longe since soe much decayed for want of Repayre as that the same became totally ruined and the parishioners thereof inforced to bee petitioned to the then Deane and Prebends for the use of a Chappel - parte of theire Cathedrall as theire parishe Church; which beinge graunted to them And the other parish Church beinge alsoe neere the said Cathedrall

it was Convenient for the said parishioners in one body to resorte to the said Cathedrall it selfe where is a Large and spatious place with verie good accomodacons for that purpose. And in the afternoone they have used to resorte to their owne parish Churches and there did heare divine service and weare Catechized and instructed in the principal grounds of religion by sufficient Ministers provided by the peticoners and their predecessors. Divine service constantly read in the said parish Churches due tymes and when any Communions are there the Comunicants after the Comunion received, so to repaire to the Sermon in the Cathedrall. And if any disorders grow uppon the Sabbath Dayes in the said Cittie either by frequentinge of Alehowses or otherwise as is pretended by the said Citties peticon the now peticoners have not bynn made acquainted therewith and if they had they would have used their best Endeavours for reformacon thereof.

It is true the tythes of the said Cittie weare Longe since appropriated to the said Cathedrall Church, soe there is no endowment belonginge to either of the said Churches or Chappells, yet the peticoners and their predecessors have beene soe Carefull to provide able men to serve the said Cures as that they have allowed to the one of them for that and other services of that Church about 50^{li} per Ann, and to the other about 40^{li} per ann, besides Many other benefitts which they receave from the peticoners in renewinge Leases they hould from the said Church and otherwise. By meanes whereof able men, Maisters of Artes and very good preachers have accepted of the said Cures and doe dilligently and Carefully attend and performe the same.

And the said Chappelries are also sufficiently supplyed with able men and one of them hath at least 20^{li} per Ann for that and other Services of the Church. And the peticoners Cannott for the present encrease either of theire Stipends from the said impropriacons because they are in Lease for divers yeares to come.

The peticoners doe repayre the said Chappel of theire Cathedrall as aforesaid, but the other of the said Churches and the said two Chappells of ease ought to bee repayred by the inhabitants and parishioners thereof.

The persons of Estate whoe dwell in the Prebends Houses have noe howses in the Cittie. And would not fixe their dwelling at Ely but for the Coveniency of those Lodgings, neither are theare above 2 men of Estate that inhabitt theare and those Justices of the peace very necessarie for governinge the Cittie and Isle of Ely.

The peticoners doe humbly offer the premisses to your Lordshipps Consideracon and doe humbly submitt themselves to your direccons concerninge any thinge herein before menconed.

And shall ever pray &c

Wm. ffuller.
Ra. Brownrigg.
Elizaeus Burges.

To remove innovations & superstition.

Fowler and Canton appear to have engaged Ewesby Andrewes, Counsellor at Law, to take care of their interests, and on the 3rd August he wrote a friendly letter to Dean Fuller, informing him of the course which affairs were taking.

Mr. Deane,

We have moved the Lords for a day; there Lordshipps pleased to signify to us that they have Intentment to take a course for a generall reformacon of the manner of service and the circumstances of tyme & place, as allso of a fitting enlargment of allowances to Curates, of wch wee shall reape our particuler benefitt, and have promised that if this bee not effected by the beginninge of the tearme wee shall thenbe heard in this when wee attend that other cause concerninge the ffeofees. My Clyants upon this have left the towne and trusted me to give you this Civill notice that you hinder not your owne affaires by giving further present attendance att this tyme on this business, & so farewell.

Your frend
E. Andrewes.

This notification was somewhat belated, for the Clerk to the Parliaments had already, on the 22nd July, issued an order calling the parties together on the second day of August, the day before that on which Ewesby Andrewes had written his letter to the Dean.

Jovis xxij° die Julij 1641.

It is this day ordered by the Right honnble the Lords Comittees for peticons in the high Courte of Parliament That the Cause dependinge before their Lordshipps between the Inhabitants of the Cittie of Ely and the Deane and Chapter of the Cathedrall Church of Ely shall bee heard on Munday the second day of August next. At which tyme William Hytch, Thomas Wyborow, Clarkes; Thomas ffowler, Thomas Canton, Robert Arkenstall, ffrauncis Ballard, John ffoxe, William Cooper, William Anger, John Taylor, Robert Anger, John Grymmer, Thomas Reyner, William Gotobed Junr., William Austen, Robert Searle, Jonas Dunch & Robert Rogers shall uppon notice hereof attend their Lordshipps at the tyme appointed to testifie their knowledge of the Matters in the peticon of the said inhabitants of Ely sett forth.

Jo. Browne.
Cleric. Parliamentore.

Parliament had indeed the "Intentment to take a course for the generall reformacon" of services in the churches and for the best part of twelve months they pressed their point. On the 1st June in 1642 the two Houses submitted to the King at York their Nineteen Propositions, of which number eight was couched in the following terms.

> That your Majesty will be pleased to consent that such a reformation be made of the Church government and liturgy as both Houses of Parliament shall advise; wherein they intend to have consultations with divines, as is expressed in their declaration to that purpose; and that your Majesty will contribute your best assistance to them for raising of a sufficient maintenance for preaching ministers throughout the kingdom; and that your Majesty will be pleased to give your consent to laws for taking away of innovations and superstition and of pluralities and against scandalous ministers.

No endowment.

The complaint that the two parish churches were unendowed was justified Both had arisen from the monastic establishment and the tythes were appropriated to the Sacrist of the monastery for the support of his office. For centuries the parishioners of Holy Trinity had been accommodated in the nave of the Cathedral, where the parish had been known as that of the Holy Cross. Possibly with the growth of the town this arrangement was found to be inconvenient, and a lean-to church was built abutting on the north side of the nave of the Cathedral. This in turn proved unsatisfactory. The parishioners complained that it was too little and was also "verie uncomelye & noysome"; moreover the Cathedral itself was "bothe darkened & made verie unholesome for wante of thorrowe ayre" by the lean-to building which blotted out the windows of the nave. Since the dissolution of the monastery the Lady Chapel had not served the purpose for which it was built, and in 1566 Dean Andrew Perne granted the use of this building to the parishioners, at the same time demolishing the lean-to church of St. Cross. Henceforth the Lady Chapel was known as the parish church of the Holy Trinity and so it remained for over four hundred years.

The parish church of St. Mary seems always to have been distinct from the monastic establishment, but both the parishes were heavily reliant upon the brethren for the cure of souls. In 1250 Bishop Hugh de Northwold had founded the Chantry on the Green on the site of the present house, and it was the Chaplains of this establishment who served the cure of the two parish churches. With the dissolution of the monastery the two churches had been appropriated to the Dean & Chapter, who had provided priests to carry out the services formerly supplied by the chaplains of the Chantry. That these services were not considered by the parishioners to be adequate or suitable is clear from the petition advanced by the two men Fowler and Canton. Of particular concern to the Puritans was the evident inadequacy of the arrangements for provision of sermons, the chief means by which instruction might be given.

Commissioners at the Dolphin.

A copy of the reply which the Dean & Chapter had made was passed to the petitioners in Ely, who carefully studied the assertions made by the Dean and noted in the margin of the document the points which they no doubt were prepared to advance before the Lords Commissioners. They also drew up a list of the witnesses they would call — substantially the names of the men mentioned in the order made by the Lords on 22nd July, but with one significant difference. The name at the head of their list was that of Mr. Cromwell. There is however no indication as to whether or not he actually attended the enquiry. It is possible that the outcome was a further investigation conducted at the Dolphin in Ely, for the Dean & Chapter account book has an entry under date of 29 Oct 1641 "Spent at the said Commission at the Dolphin for the Diet of ye Commissioners & witnesses ut per billam   02.02.11d." The Cathedral authorities had evidently engaged the Ely attorney Philip Attlesey and paid him "for his Charges in fouler's Suit   £1.0.0d."

The Ely petitioners' case can clearly be made out from their marginal remarks on the copy of the answer made by the Dean & Chapter. To Dean Fuller's statement that the Cathedral authorities had granted the use of the Lady Chapel to Holy Trinity parishioners they retort:- "They tooke downe the parish Church & sold or made use of the materialls." The services were "not reade in due time" and the "Sermon most done att those tymes with great disturbance."

There was, perhaps, justification for this last remark. Probably since the monastic days both parishes had been required to repair to the Cathedral nave to hear sermons. An earlier generation had complained that the seats in the sermon place were "low & narrow and were fashioned like hogg-troughs & horse-mangers" and they were removed. From that time individuals were permitted to bring their own seats, but although the sermon place was large, the space within which the preacher could be heard was limited, and there was a good deal of jostling and manoeuvering to bring the seats within hearing distance of the preacher.

The way to prevent the "disorders growing uppon the Sabbath dayes by the frequenting of Alehouses" (a state of affairs of which the Dean disclaimed any knowledge) would be in the opinion of the petitioners "to bring the Sermons to the parish churches".

But perhaps the greatest cause of the evident dissatisfaction of the parishioners was the absolute reliance on the Cathedral body for the provision of priests who should be responsible for the cure of souls of either parish. Although the Dean claimed that in addition to the stipends which they received the two ministers had a revenue from certain leases which they held of the Chapter, and "Masters of Arts & very good preachers have accepted of the Cures", it is evident that the petitioners were not prepared to accept this situation as satisfactory. "The many services they doe to the Cathedrall hynders the due Services to the parishes in their proper tymes" since "both are servants to the Cathedral church" and were in fact "two of ye quire".

Was the criticism of the two ministers entirely justified? William Hitch, the parson of Holy Trinity, was in fact Precentor of the Cathedral and his attendance at the choral services there would occupy a good deal of his time. He was also a master at the King's School, where he received a salary of £16.3.4d. per annum, considerably more than his stipend as a parish priest. But his concern for his parish church appears to have been most praiseworthy and he seems to have earned the genuine regard of his church people. He certainly conducted the parish affairs in an extremely efficient manner, as is evidenced by his churchwardens' accounts. What were his qualities as a preacher we have no means of knowing, but it is possible that his concern was more for the performance of the "opus Dei" in the cathedral than for the exposition of Puritan doctrine.

St. Mary's church was perhaps not so fortunate in its minister; Thomas Wiborow was indeed "one of the quire". He had been appointed Lay Clerk in 1636 and was placed in charge of the parish church in 1640. He too was a master at the King's School, but as the petitioners pointed out, rather disparagingly, he was "but a deacon".

The curates who served the two chapels of ease at Chettisham and Stuntney no doubt devoted even less time to their cures. They received a salary of £1.6.8d per annum, a mere pittance even in the seventeenth century, and it is evident that their curacys were of secondary importance and merely supplemented the income which they gained in Ely. Robert Hinde had had the cure of Stuntney for almost fifty years, but since 1604 had also been under-master at the King's School in Ely. The salary of the chaplain at Chettisham, Jonathan Westwood, was supplemented by wages for payment of which the inhabitants had been made responsible. When the churchwardens returned their bill at the Bishop's visitation made at Midsummer 1638 they presented "Nath Fox for that he being a surgener in our hamlett of Churcham denyeth in peremptory and sawsy manner either to rate himself or be rated by others towards the curates wages for reading prayers and preaching there."

The Lady Chapel.

The contention that the two churches had been allowed to fall into disrepair may indeed have been well founded, but so far as St. Mary's was concerned only the chancel was the responsibility of the Dean & Chapter as impropriators. The same thing applied to Chettisham, but the Rectory of Stuntney, although impropriate by the capitular body, was leased to the Steward family, who farmed the tithes, and it was Sir Simeon Steward who was responsible for the chancel of that church.

Under the arrangement by which the use of the Lady Chapel had been granted to the Holy Trinity parishioners the Dean & Chapter were to be responsible for "the vaultes, walles, rooffes, sydes, leades, coveringes & windowes", whilst the parishioners should "at there propper coste & chardges make all the Pews, Seates & Deskes & the Table for the mynistracion of the Lordes Supper there". In practice it would seem that the parishioners were concerned with interior decoration of the church. In 1576 they spent "vjd for paynting the wall before the Communion table." In 1581 they expended twenty pence and in the next year five shillings and four pence for the same purpose. It is evident that the sanctuary which occupied the nine eastern bays was then enclosed with a screen. Traces of mural decoration are much more distinct in this part of the church than elsewhere. The screen itself was removed in 1585.

> "Paid to Scott and Baly for takinge
> down the skrene in the church   viij s
> For help in taking down the skrene   vjd "

Two years earlier, i.e. in 1583, there had been a "charge of ye removinge of the pullpet iijs vd" and again in 1585 "for makinge the pulpet higher & the tester xs."

No doubt the parishioners had found that the structure of the Lady Chapel, designed as it was for monastic worship, was ill-fitted for their use. They had therefore demolished the screen and set the pulpit much nearer the east end, thus reducing the extent of the sanctuary to meet the requirements of a parish church and at the same time increasing almost twofold the space available for the provision of seating for the congregation.

Whether such structural alteration had been envisaged when the use of the chapel was granted by Dean Perne, or whether there had over the years grown up the practice of looking to the parishioners for the maintenance of the fabric in part, it is clear that Dean Fuller's contention that the capitular body "doe repayre the Chappell of their Cathedral" was hotly disputed by the petitioners. They claimed it was "repaired by the parish when the King came thither (in 1636) by Watsonn, Churchwarden, by the command of the Archdeacon." And in spite of this, they added with evident feeling, it is "insufferably cold".

Persons of great estate.

The final grievance expressed in the petition concerned the letting of prebendal lodgings to "Persons of great estate," to the detriment of the Ely ratepayers. The Dean's answer that these buildings provided accommodation for Justices of the Peace and other responsible men is merely begging the question. What the Ely citizens complained of was that the burden of the rates was not shared by the College, which was extra-parochial, and whilst they were apparently content that the Cathedral establishment should enjoy such immunity, they strongly objected, on this and many subsequent occasions, to the extension of the freedom from local rating to the men of substance who were merely tenants of the prebendal lodgings.

As early as the year 1616, when a visitation of the Cathedral was made, the Chancellor had "exhorted the Dean & Prebendaries to be vigilant & careful that the service of Almighty God in that church be not neglected, but dutifully performed with all care & diligence, and that forasmuch as some harde reporte & speeches are spred abroad that some of the prebendaries houses ther are lett out to some supposed & suspected to be usurers & some to other of evil name, fame & credits & of suspected conversations, he willed and desired the prebendaries to be more careful in placing any in their houses and that they would remove any such for avoiding of scandal."

During the next two and a half centuries this feeling of resentment against the letting of prebendal houses was never long absent from the minds of the ratepayers of the parishes and during the eighteenth century brought frequent wrangling between the college and the town. When, as sometimes happened, employees of the Cathedral foundation, or their families, living in the College were reduced in circumstances either by their own actions or by the death of the breadwinner the parishioners of Holy Trinity found themselves called upon to make provision for them. Since no rates had ever been paid by these people, nor any on their behalf, the Holy Trinity ratepayers complained bitterly of the injustice which they suffered. It must be confessed that successive Deans & Chapters usually took up an attitude which did nothing to relieve the situation.

Dean Fuller's contention is typical of the evasiveness with which the ratepayers' complaints were usually met.

Many dark corners.

What was the immediate outcome of the Commission in Ely is not clear. Perhaps the improvement which the petitioners urged became sunk in the "Intentment to take a course for the generall reformacon in the manner of service" which had been expressed in Ewesby Andrewes' letter to the Dean. On every possible occasion during the next few years in their negotiations with the King Parliament pursued the question of church reform.

In the "Declaration of the Houses on Church Reform" made on the 8th April 1642 they had urged "Consultation with godly & learned divines" who would "use their utmost endeavour to establish learned and preaching ministers, with a good and sufficient maintenance throughout the whole kingdom, wherein many dark corners are miserably destitute of the means of salvation, and many poor ministers want necessary provision." And in the Propositions presented to the King at Oxford on 24th November 1644 it was pressed upon His Majesty "to give his royal assent to the Bill for the suppression of innovations in churches and chapels" and "for the better advancement of the preaching of God's Holy Word."

But it was not until 1646, two years after the outbreak of hostilities, that the resolution to remove the powers of the Bishops was brought into effect and all bishoprics were suppressed. Deans & Chapters survived for another three years before they too succumbed to the Puritan attack and in April 1649 order was made for the sale of their lands.

However, when in the same year the Parliamentary Commissioners made a survey which covered the Rectory of Ely they noted that in addition to the ten pounds apiece which was due to the parish clergy it should "also be lawfull for the two chaplains to receive and take all oblations & offerings of two pence of every communicant in the said several parishes at Easter & Whitsontide & to enjoy the said Offerings to ye said Chaplains without the interruption of any person." These oblations "amongst other things granted by Oliver Cromwell Esqr., late Farmer of ye said Rectory, and by Daniel Wigmore, late Archdeacon of Ely" had been granted to Richard Ponsonby of Ely, Tanner, who is elsewhere described as "servant to Mr. Cromwell". The increase in the remuneration to the parish clergy would not seem to be very substantial. The oblations of St. Mary's amounted to something like £2 per annum. Mr. Hitch, at Holy Trinity, would receive at least twice that amount, since his parish was very much larger and covered two thirds of the city of Ely.

The inhabitants named.

The two petitions advanced by Thomas Fowler and Thomas Canton had the support of many of the inhabitants and they secured the signatures of some hundred individuals on a parchment sheet which is headed:-

"The severall names of the Inhabitants of the Cittey of Ely who perticoned to the honble house of Parliamt for redresse of the saide abuses before by them expressed by these presence."

Of the individuals concerned thirty-five make their marks, but no fewer than sixty-three were capable of signing their names, an extremely high rate of literacy which must indicate that they were representative of the more substantial citizens. Thomas Fowler was the owner of the Homestall, the farm which embraces most of the hamlet of Chetisham. William Waller, who drew up the list, was an attorney; so was William Adam. Gabriel Legat was churchwarden of St. Mary's and Roman Kisby parish constable. Jonas Dunch was churchwarden at Stuntney. Thomas Gotobed lived on the site of the King's Arms; he held £12 of the parish stock. Edward Bate and Robert Aungier held between them £39. John Clarke always appended "gent" to his signature, presumably to distinguish himself from the other John Clarke who always affixed "potter" to his name. Representative of the tradesmen was Clement Hind the brewer; the brewery he founded passed from one to another of his descendants to the middle years of the present century. He was brother to the curate who served the chapelry of Stuntney. There was Valentine Mott, whose boatwright's business flourished over at Babylon; and another potter, Thomas Lamb. John Pigott was a fellmonger — the Pigotts owned half a dozen properties in Ely, among them the residence in Broad Street which was later to become the "Three Blackbirds", now threatened with demolition. Richard Ponsonby the tanner lived on the site of the public library; servant to Oliver Cromwell he was later to take over the lease of the Rectory of Ely from his master and eventually to become one of the sequestrators of the Dean & Chapter lands. John Grimmer was son of Thomas Grimmer the man who had made the new door for the Bishop's prison a few years earlier. John had been a cathedral chorister and his name may be seen carved on the wall of Bishop Alcock's chapel in the cathedral.

William Waller, Junior, had been busy securing signatures from the bottom of the town. To William Waller the attorney he passed a list inscribed "To his ever loving father William Waller att Ely delever this. The names of the inhabitants in Castle hive ward". Of the sixteen signatories only eight could write their names, the remainder make their marks and among them is the distinctive ₣Ţ₮ "mark of Edward Poule", the man who three years earlier had led the commoners in their attacks on the river banks. On his release from Newgate he had returned to Ely and was living in the Castlehithe quarter of the town by the Annesdale quayside.

The severall names of the Inhabitants of the
Colledge of Chichester presented to the Court fflete of
Portland for redresse of the said abuses
before by them aggreeued by thes
presentes

Phi Rearson
william walkar

Thomas Brymer
Richard Darrell
Jonas Dunty
Godfrey woosham
Browne Pollard
Dorothy Cannon
william Tarbox
George Turkinton
william Bross
Thomas Tille
Thomas H lamot
Roberto Osenterton
Dallentin mott
Symon Stone
Symon Mott
Thomas Lambe potter
William Mott
Andrew Bosloys
Jospet wilo
Joseph Alpin
John moovis
Beniamen Musson
fennet + Dinty
Robart R Gotobed.
Gervill Gaynot
Thomas Hack
ffrauncis hunty
Christofer Cobb
Jonas Dunty
Richard Ponsonby
Edward Clobbe
his marke
Jarnot P Jordan
John H Harrison
garg Bosato
william Gurdin
John A Gabnt
David Dale

Thomas Fedwerd
Robert Iohn Snow
william Lant
Andrew Nifall
Richard Foss
Edw Gspanland
Clemon Hind
Wilof Goodman
John + Wright
william Cubles
John Giggot
Coryard Thompson
Edward Tafbill
george Thomson
william Sayer
Thomas Sayer
Robt Moss
William Grayman
James Poyo

william Sibbe
John S Anngiar
Tobias gotobed
Harry J Wfall
Thomas n briff
Thomas Lynce
Gabrill Lefat

william V Anger
Thomas Palmer
William Cooper
Robert Ranyor
william Smith
Thomas Collin
Henry Timgoys
his marke
Robert Day Gunstop
John Clarke got
Willey X Gotobed
Thomas Gotobed
Nicholas Munzorff
Nicholas Pay
John E Legall
william Cobbed
Regt Cobbed
Edward Bato

34

Phi: Izacson
Willyam Wallar
John Grymer
Richard Oldcorne
Jonas Dunch

Godfrey Woolsonn

ffrancys ᚠᚠ Ballard
Jeremy Cannon
William Tucke
Percye Turkinton
William Scott
Thomas Disse
   his mrke
Thomas ⊢⊣ Cannot
Robert Chaderton
Valentin Mott
Thomas ffoxe
Thomas Mott
Thomas Lambe potter
Willyam Mott
Andrewe Bezleye
Ƌhis mke
Jesper Adkin

John Morris
Beniamin Musson
James ┬ Dunch

Robart ℞ Gotobed

Cherhill Haynes
Thomas Leach
ffrancis Duntch
Christopher Cobb
Jonas Dunch
Richard Ponsonbe
Edward Cobbe
   his marke
James ◖Jordan

John ℲⳆ Harrison
Georg Beesele
William /⋀\ harvie
John ✕ Gaunt
David ⬤ Gie

Thomas Andrewes
Owen Lavender
William Larett
Andrew ⊘ Nitall
Richard Rose

Edw ⌒⋀ Aspenland

Clement Hind
Miles ᷆Goodman

John ⚹ ⊗ Wright
William Siblie
John ⊓ piggot
   ⊔
Richard Compton

Edward ✝ cattelle
Henry Thomson
William Sayer
Thomas Sayer
Robt Bell

William Seagrave

James Daye

William Siblye

John ⓺ Aungiar
   ⊘
Tobias Gotobed

Henry Pepall
      Gabrill Legat
Roman kisbe ⌐
Thomas Hynd ┌

   his marke
William ↰⌐Angier
Thomas Rainer
William ⊣⊤ Cooper
Robert Aungier
William Smith
Thomas Collin

Henry Tinggeye

   his marke
Robert ⌒Daye
? ᶜSivertop

John Clarke get.

Phillip ⋈ Gotobed

Thomas ⟍ Gotobed

Nicholas Aunger
Nicholas Day

John ⊥ Legatt

Willm ⟩ Gotobed

Rich Gotobed

Edward Bate

The names of the
inhabitants in Castle
hive ward.

Willyam Wallar
Thomas Baxter

Joseph Jarman

Edward Poule

John Johnson

Willyam Cutrich

Willyam Dixson

Christopher ffishar
John kilborne

Robbard Bishope

Thomas Aunger

Robt Diss
Jeremy Cutteris
John Hisson

Willyam Pigot

John Taylor

To his veri loving
ffather William
Wallar att Ely
Delever this.

The Reproached Doctrine of Ely.

Most of these men were no doubt perfectly orthodox Protestant churchmen, but one signature comes into a different category. It is that of Christopher Cobb, Layman, Minister of an United People in Ely. In 1651 he was to publish a book of his sermons under the title "The Reproached Doctrine of Ely, the Sect every where spoken against." "Judged of all, known of none; a shame to be for it, a danger to be of it, a sin to be in it." He reveals that these people "in this present year 1651 both Minister and People after twenty years faithful Service in the Gospel stand indicted for an unlawful and most uncivil Assembly gathered and united contrary to the Laws of the Commonwealth. What plots and contrivances are there on foot to break us a pieces, if the Lord prevent not. What stirrings and waitings for our haltings. It hath been no small Mercy the peaceable Government we have lived under, we have had Liberty and Peace to meet together; it is more then was afforded in my day, it cost me dearer."

His sermons reveal the teaching of a very real Hell-fire and he castigates his congregation unmercifully:-

> Alas! you that go and come and sit here as pictures, and are no more sensible then the stones in the wall; all this is nothing to you. And I am wondering sometimes how it is possible you should thus sleep away your time and never consider you are going apace to Hell and destruction, but like the smith's dog, sleep quietly, though the sparks fly about your ears."

Christopher Cobb's attacks on the established Church appear to be based on the conviction that the ministers of religion were not fulfilling their duties adequately. "I have known some Ministers myself that have been preaching these thirty years and not a man converted by them. Many preach indeed and they take the charge of the people, as they say; but how long? Until another hundred pound a year comes and then they are gone."

His attacks on the church however were not confined to criticism of the establishment. It is obvious that, together with many of the Presbyterians, he had been bitterly disappointed at the manner in which the question of church reform had not been pursued with greater vigour. In his sermon on "Man's Backwardness to the Lord's House" he writes:- "But how long we linger, and the building of this house is neglected! I remember the motioning and stirring towards this work was up in some hearts at least twenty years since; but the Bishops they got up and crushed all the tender buddings, that the work ceased, and since this Parliament the Lord hath graciously procured Liberty to be proclaimed, a door open for this work, and many have begun to build; but they prove Houses of their own invention and contrivances, not the Lord's House."

Evidence of the existence of a more fanatical Puritan element in Ely is provided by the returns for the Bishop's visitation of Holy Trinity at Michaelmas 1638. William Wade gave evidence "that he was present and an actor on new yeeres day at ye time of ye service in ye quire when a great noyse & disturbance was made neere ye quire of the Cathedral church of Ely by ye roasting of a catt tied to a spitt by one William Smyth, and there a fier about it, whereby much people were gathered together and a great prophanation made both of ye day and ye place."

There is little doubt that this was a protest against the Bishop's re-introduction of high church practices. The poor creature would be dressed in imitation vestments of the mass and consigned to the flames. Less than a century earlier the two Protestants, Wolsey and Pigott, had been burned before the Cathedral during the Marian persecution of 1557, and no doubt some of the citizens of Ely viewed with apprehension the bishop's leaning towards Rome as they supposed. William Smith, the perpetrator of the horrible deed, was one of the signatories to the petition for the reformation of the church services — or rather, he made his mark.

Levellers.

Apart from the religious convictions of the Puritan element in Ely it is evident that some of the political opinions which were being advanced by the group of people known as the Levellers under John Lilburne had penetrated the city. Some two years later, in 1644, Lilburne was to publish his manifesto "The Free Man's Freedom Vindicated" wherein he set forth his beliefs.

"All & every particular & individual man & woman that ever breathed in the world are by nature all equal & alike in their power, dignity, authority & majesty, none of them having (by nature) any authority, dominion or magisterial power one over or above another."

These beliefs are clearly to be discerned in the opinions expressed by the Ely brazier John Gotobed. On the 12th May 1642 he was charged, on the information of John Orwell, gent, and John Bert, cordwayner, with having said in the house of Mr. James called the Griffin that "In God's estimacon theire was no respect of persons if a man's hart was right. That the Kinge had noe more to doe then these informants or himselfe. And that if we would not be ruled wee should be ruled very shortley. And he further demanded of these informants "What was the Kinge more than wee were." Such dangerous speech was too much for the Justice, William March, good Parliament man though he was. In July of the same year John Gotobed was languishing in the Bishop's prison at Ely.

However, political opinions expressed in the Griffin were not always favourable to Parliament. In 1650 the proprietor William Seagrave, was prosecuted "for keepinge disorder in his house uppon the Sabboth day by drinckinge & singing Cavaliere songs." No doubt reaction was setting in against the recent execution of the King. The Griffin had frequent changes of name. It was formerly known as The Antilope and acquired its name The Griffin at the beginning of the 17th century. After the restoration of the monarchy in 1660, when Bishop Wren was released from prison and returned to his diocese, the inn celebrated the event by re-naming the house "The Mitre", and it was over a century before the name was again changed, to the Chequers. The building still

The Chequers.   Photo Donald Monk

stands in Chequer Lane, but its life as an inn ceased in the late 1950s.

Joyfull Newes from the Isle of Ely.

In August of the fateful year 1642 the King raised his standard at Nottingham. The City of London, with its trained militia bands declared for Parliament and East Anglia flocked to join the Parliamentary army which as we have seen was being raised under the Earl of Essex. Cromwell sought and obtained permission from the Commons to muster volunteers in his own constituency of Cambridge. An attempt made to secure the College plate for the service of the King and to remove it to Newmarket was frustrated by the Parliamentary forces, who intercepted the Royalist sympathisers on the road. The activities of the troop of horsemen despatched to prevent money, plate and arms from falling into the hands of the King are triumphantly described in a broadsheet issued by the Parliament in September.

JOYFULL NEWES
FROM THE
ISLE OF ELY,
DECLARING *K*

The manner of the apprehending of Bishop *Wren*, and his bringing up to *London*, together with his Treasure, on Thursday the first of September, by a Company of Horsmen that went to search his house, being suspected to have store of Armes and Ammunition, attested by *George Hubbard*, dwelling at *Downham* where the Bishops Pallaee is, and now evidently appeares by his apprehension.

Declaring how a Troupe of Horse is gone into *Cambridge shire* to search the Papists Houses, among which D.*Wren* Bishop of *Ely* is like to suffer, being suspected to have store of Ammunition.

ON Munday the nine and twentieth of August a Troupe of well-affected Horsemen met together in *Cambridge-Skire* neere *Cherrie-Hinton*, with an intent to search all the Papists house, thereabouts, in which search they found but small store of armes and ammunition, at which they not a little wondered :

JOYFULL NEWES
from the
ISLE OF ELY
declaring

The manner of the apprehending of Bishop Wren, and his bringing up to London, together with his Treasure on Thursday the first of September, by a Company of Horsmen that went to search his house, being suspected to have store of Armes and Ammunition, attested by George Hubbard, dwelling at Downham where the

Bishops Pallace is, and now evidently appeares by his apprehension. Declaring how a Troupe of Horse is gone into Cambridge shire to search the Papists Houses, among which D. Wren Bishop of Ely is like to suffer, being suspected to have store of Ammunition.

ON Munday the nine and twentieth of August a Troupe of wellaffected Horsemen met together in Cambridge-Shire neere Cherrie-Hinton, with an intent to search all the Papists houses thereabouts, in which search they found but small store of armes and ammunition, at which they not a little wondered: but one among the rest told them, they had mist one of the greatest Papists, of a little one, in the whole Kingdome: and being asked who it was, he told them it was D. Wren Bishop of Ely; and that it was not improbable that the Papists had made his house their Magazine. he being the chiefe authour of these trubles in this Kingdome.

This being mentioned, they all agreed furnish themselves accordingly with powder and shot, and forthwith to march thither, purposing to search out all his treachery, withall promising to clip his wings, if they could catch him.

Moreover, it is reported by the Attester of this Relation that the Bishop doth countenance all outrages whatsoever, nay murder itselfe; for his Steward lately kild a poore man for demanding money for his labour, who after many reproachfull and menacing words, had his brains beaten out, and the Steward now lives under the Bishops protection.

Likewise the said Bishop hath entertained all the deboist Cavaliers that inhabited in the Colledge and townes, being fittest for his purpose.

The Island of it selfe is very strong; but the chiefe Officers thereof are for the most part of the Bishops faction his power having beene formerly so great and uncontrouleable in the Island: But there is great hope that they will stand firme to the Parliament: and the rather, because they hope that the Parliament will give them their Fennes againe, and curbe the undertakers, the countrey being almost undone for want of them.

The Isle is furnished with store of good horses and able men, but in their discipline very rude, for want of expert Commanders. This is the truth,

Attested by George Hubbard,
inhabitant of Downham
in the Isle of Ely.

The truth and certainty of this attestation is now most evident: for now after this relation of the Horsemen that were sent to search the Prelates house, he was brought up to London, together with great store of money, which the Priest had gathered together to further the designes of the male-content and ill-affected Clergie, as is probably coniectured. The just summe of his treasure is not yet certainly known. Ex aliis alia quaeras, if thou thy selfe hast better.

Iconoclasts.

Whether any armed resistance was offered by the Royalist sympathisers in Ely is doubtful. Apparently some action had been contemplated and efforts were made to put the Cathedral and precincts into a state of defence. "Railes, posts and pailes" were put up in the College, and the Porta, the great gateway which stands at the entrance to the precincts, was strengthened with iron work, perhaps window bars or re-inforcement of the great timber gates. The Deanery, now the Bishop's house, received similar attention, and work of some kind was done on the great doors at the west end of the Cathedral. But there is no record that these defences were ever put to the test. It is true that when the woodwork of the great doors which open from the Galilee Porch to the nave at the west end required some repair in 1850 there were found embedded in the timber several heavy pieces of lead, splayed and flattened, which might have been fired from a musket. But there is no reason to conclude that these, if they are musket balls, were discharged during the Civil War.

Certainly no such violence was offered to the Cathedral as was presented at Peterborough when the Parliamentary forces visited that city on their way to the reduction of Crowland in 1643 under the leadership of Cromwell himself. In spite of special orders that the soldiery should "do no injury to the church" they broke open the doors and destroyed the organ and monuments, among them those of the two queens Catherine and Mary. But Ely, of course, as early as 1541 had been purged of all "Romish & idolatrous" elements by its reforming bishop, Thomas Goodrich, that "zealous forwarder of the Reformation" in the days of the Protector Somerset. The Bishop's injunctions to the clergy, dated at Ely 21st October 1541, had been "to see that all Images, Relicks, Table Monuments of Miracles, Shrines etc. be so totally demolished and obliterated with all speed & diligence that no remains or memory might be found of them for the future."

Which injunctions, Bentham tells us, "were executed with such speed, secrecy and punctuality in his Cathedral and other churches in the Diocese of Ely that no traces remain of many famous shrines and altars which formerly were the objects of frequent resort." It is ironical that of the two ancient monumental brasses remaining in the Cathedral one should be of this same Thomas Goodrich who had swept away so much church ornament and wrought such havoc amidst the magnificence of the Lady Chapel of his own cathedral.

Come down, Mr. Hitch!

Perhaps it was the memory of the desecration of Peterborough which prompted Cromwell to write the famous letter to the Precentor at Ely quoted by Clement Walker in his "Sufferings of the Clergy".

"Lest the souldiers should in any tumultuary or disorderly way attempt the reformation of the Cathedral Church, I require you to forbear altogether your choir service, so unedifying and offensive - and this as you shall answer for it if any disorder should arise therefrom.

I advise you to catechise and read and expound the Scriptures to the people; not doubting but the Parliament, with the advice of the

Assembly of Divines, will direct you further. I desire your sermons, too, where usually they have been, but more frequent.

Your loving friend,
Oliver Cromwell''.

"Notwithstanding this letter" Walker goes on to tell us, "Mr. Hitch continued to officiate as before. Upon which Cromwell with a party of soldiers attended by the rabble, came into church in the time of divine service, with his hat on, and directing himself to Mr. Hitch, said 'I am a man under authority and am commanded to dismiss this assembly.' Mr. Hitch proceeded with the service, at which Cromwell, laying his hand on his sword in a passion, bade Mr. Hitch to 'leave off his fooling and come down' and so drove out the whole congregation.''

There are stories still current in Ely of the drilling of the Cromwellian Ironsides on St. Mary's green and even of the stabling of horses in the Lady Chapel, but it is doubtful whether there is any foundation for them. We cannot suppose that Ely was so short of stable accommodation that the latter course would be necessary or convenient.

The church registers hold no record of any who might have been killed in armed conflict. John Brown "miles" was buried on the 13th June 1645, and William Graston "miles" on the 2nd November 1649, but these are the only recorded instances of the burial of soldiers, and there is no reason to suppose that the interments were the result of any military activity in Ely.

In the King's service.

We know the names of several men from the neighbourhood who served in the wars. After the Restoration of the Monarchy in 1662 a grateful country granted a pension of £5 per annum to certain men for their "good & faithfull service & wounds received in his late Majesty's service". To cover the three years from 1662 to 1665 Thomas Kilburne of Ely was paid a pension of £15 by the Treasurer for Pensions in the Isle of Ely; this charge was levied on the parishes. Thomas Kilburne had been baptized at Holy Trinity on the 26th November 1620 of parents living in Annesdale. For many years the lane running at the rear of the present Castelhythe was known as Kilburne's Lane, and the signature of his father John Kilborne is included amongst those of the residents of Castelhythe on the list submitted by William Waller junior in 1642.

Charles Dench (or Dunch) was the subject of dispute between the county of Buckingham and the Isle. He was born at Stuntney in 1619 and at the beginning of hostilities, when he was aged 23 he enlisted and served in the Royalist cause under the command of Colonel John Russell. Having been wounded during the wars he settled at Fenny Stratford in Buckinghamshire as a tailor and in 1662 Sir John Russell wrote to the Buckinghamshire authorities on his behalf:-

"Sir, This barers povertie togeather with his ingagements in the King's service during the time of the warre in my Regiment induces mee to make a supplycation to you that if it bee possible hee may receave by your favour some augmentation to that little allowance hee hath alreadie obtaind in which you will doe an act of charitie and very much

oblige
Your most humble servant
John Russell.

Woeburne Abbie
the 1st of October 1662.

He was granted a pension of £5 per annum. Three years later however, the Justices of Buckinghamshire wrote to their counterparts in the Isle.

To his Majesties Justices of the peace in the Isle of Ely.
Buckes.
Wee whose names are hereunto subscribed, Justices of the peace for the County of Buckes, Doe Certifie that Charles Dench of ffenystratford in this County, Laborer, is a very poore person and much unable by reason of his wounds received in his Majesties service to doe any business towards his Lively hoode & that hee hath since his Majesties happy Restoration bin allowed a pention in this County ffor his good & faithfull service & wounds received, but uppon a Revew of our Pentioners finding him the said Charles Dench & severall others of them to have gone into his said Late Majesties service from other Counties & soe ought to have pentions from the said Counties of which they went in to the said Service, wee have therefore taken away theire Pentions here, not knowing but they may alsoe have obtained pentions in the said Counties & if the said Charles Dench be not now one of your pentioners wee recomend him to you to that purpose as a most ffitt person for a Pention, he goeing (as we have bin duly informed) from Stuntney in the Isle of Ely att ffirst into his Majesties service. In Wittness whereof wee have here unto sett our hands & seales this sixt day of August in the 16th yeare of his Majesties Raigne.

An Chester.	Tho Stafford.
Tho Hackett.	Brett Norton.
	Tho Duncomb.
	Thomas Farrar.

44

Thomas Steward, from the Manor House of Stuntney, took up the matter on behalf of his fellow townsman. Writing from Stuntney on the 6th of October 1664 he addressed a letter to his brother-in-law William March, who was one of the Justices at Ely.

"Brother March,
This bearer Charles Dench whoe went formerly out of our Towne into the late Kings Army & served under the Comand of Col John Russell as by his Certificat appereth And had formerly a pencon allowed him for such his service in Buckinghamshire, but lately upon a Reviewe taken there they finde him to goe from Stuntney & not out of their County and therefore have taken away their pencon from him there & have recomended him to us as by their Certificate appeareth. I therefore desire you to doe mee & him the kindnesse to help him to that pencon wch was allowed to John Dench his kinsman while hee lived, wch wilbe no further charge to the Isle then what was imposed upon it before and therein you will much oblige
Your respective Brother & servant
Tho. Steward.

ᴧᴴ
I Andrue fell knu that charls dench
weant out of Stuntney with roobard March.

Charles Dench was Borne in Stuntney
& Lived theire in Stuntney.
Witnesse my hand

John Piggott.

Divided loyalties.
The Ely magistrates granted Thomas Steward's request, but the Isle proved less generous than Buckinghamshire; Charles Dunch was awarded a pension of £4 per annum. It is clear that the Dunch family were very much committed to the conflict, for as is revealed in Thomas Steward's letter another member of the family had also been in receipt of a pension.
A glance at the background of these Royalist soldiers will serve to illustrate the way in which families were divided in their loyalties during the war. Both Kilburnes and Dunches signed the Puritan petition for the reformation of church services, and William March, who secured Charles Dunch's pension, was a good Parliament man. Robert March, with whom Charles Dunch "went out of Stuntney" was of the same family.
The Russells were active on both sides. William, first Duke of Bedford, commanded the Parliamentary cavalry at Edgehill. It is true that in 1643 he abandoned the Parliamentary cause and joined the King at Oxford in an attempt to induce Charles to comply with Parliament's demands, but his defection was of short duration and he quickly returned to his earlier allegiance.
Though there were some Puritans who from the beginning sought to destroy

the monarchy the vast majority were motivated by their dislike of Charles and his High Church policy. The notes which Zachary Grey made on Samuel Butler's famous satire "Hudibras" illustrate the agonizing choice which was presented to many of them and the way in which they strove to justify their actions.

"The Presbyterians in all their wars against the King maintained still that they fought for him; for they pretended to distinguish his political person from his natural one. For his political person, they said, must be with the parliament, though his natural person was at war with them."

In the Earl of Essex's commission the King was named, although that commission placed Essex in command of the forces recruited specifically to oppose the Royalist cause and Charles had issued the proclamation declaring him a traitor.

Butler's satirical lines make the same point.

> For as we make war for the King
> Against himself, the self-same thing
> Some will not stick to swear we do
> For God & for religion too.

And again:-

> Did they not swear, at first, to fight
> For the King's safety & his right?
> And after marched to find him out
> And charg'd him home with horse & foot.
> But yet still had the confidence
> To swear it was in his defence.

A strong fastness.

After the outbreak of war, with Cromwell's involvement in the military engagements, the city of Ely saw little of him. In 1643 he was one of the Sequestrators appointed in Cambridgeshire for seizing the estates of "certain notorious delinquents (among them Bishop Wren) who had raised arms against Parliament". But in the next year he left Ely to take up residence at Westminster, where Madame Cromwell joined him in 1646. His lease of the Rectory was sublet to his servant Richard Ponsonby, who held it for several years. Eventually it came into the hands of the Archdeacon, Daniel Wigmore, and so passed to his heirs.

In May 1645 an attempt was made by one of the King's Captains to betray Ely to the Royalists and Cromwell returned to the city charged with the task of securing the Isle for Parliament. He raised "twenty barrells of powder, bullet & match; 2000 men, two sakers & four drakes" but does not appear to have made use of them in the Isle. A rumour that the King was at Peterborough drew him to St. Ives, but he still left the Isle strongly garrisoned.

Clement Walker in his "Compleat History of Independency" which he wrote in 1648, just before the exclusion of the Presbyterians from the House of Commons, gives a vivid description of conditions in the Isle. He was bitterly opposed to Cromwell, the Independents and the Army.

"Since the revolt of some of their Ships hath almost made them hopeless of transportation to foreign Plantations the schismatical Grandees have made Col. Walton (Brother-in-law to Cromwell) Governour of Lyn, Boston and Crowland, and of all that level of morasse Ground in the Isles of Ely, Holland and Marshland, which they can lay under water at pleasure; it is a plentiful and strong fastness, able to feed 40,000 men, besides the ordinary Inhabitants; there are but three passes to enter it, over three Bridges, upon which they have or may build Forts for their defence & may from thence invade the adjacent Country at pleasure, being themselves free from incursions; or they may (if they list) break down the said Bridges. These places (already strong by nature) they daily fortifie by art; for which purpose great sums of money have been sent to him, and much Arms, Powder, Ammunition and Ordnance from Windsor Castle. Here (when all other helps fail) the Godly mean to take Sanctuary; this shall be their last retreat, from whence they will draw the whole Kingdom to Parly upon Articles of treaty, and enforce their peace from them at last. These are the stratagems of the Godly; these are our Saints, nowhere canonized but in the Devil's Calendar.

A parish priest.

Although Mr. Hitch had been commanded to "cease his fooling and come down" it would seem that the Cathedral services were not at this time discontinued, although the music was no doubt drastically curtailed. Robert Claxton, the organist, living in his house on the Palace Green (still standing next to the Public Library) was reduced to giving instruction as a teacher of the viols, probably to pupils of the King's School. This he continued to do throughout the Commonwealth period and with the Restoration of the Monarchy in 1660 he was restored to his position as organist, although he was then in failing health and died shortly after.

Dean Fuller had left Ely in 1645 to join Charles at Oxford. Here he preached several times before the King and in the following year was granted the Deanery of Durham, though he was never instiued. William Beale, Master of St. John's College, Cambridge, was nominated as Fuller's successor at Ely, but he too was never admitted.

We may suppose that Mr. Hitch was no longer pursuing his calling as Precentor in the Cathedral, but he was certainly assiduous in carrying out his duties as the parish priest of Holy Trinity. From his house in the Gallery, opposite the Porta and on the site later to be occupied by the King's School building, Hereward Hall, he conducted the parish affairs throughout the Commonwealth

period. He did not live to see the restoration of the music in the Cathedral; he died in the year 1659 and was succeeded, though not immediately, but his son Thomas as Minister of Holy Trinity.

For many years the house at the corner of the Gallery remained in the possession of his descendants. In 1686 it was leased to the Governors of Parson's Charity, who established a Blue Coat school in the building. Later it flourished as an inn known by the sign of the Black Swan, a name which by the middle of the 19th century had been supplanted by that of the Green Man. It was demolished in 1880 to make room for the new King's School building.

The Sequestrators.

Throughout the whole of the Commonwealth period Bishop Wren remained a prisoner in the Tower. He had been first committed to prison in 1641, and the Commons on the 6th April in the following year made an order "That Matthew Bishop of Ely shall be allowed One hundred pounds per annum." A month later he was released and returned to his palace at Little Downham, only to be again arrested in August. The arms and money he had gathered for the support of the King were secured for Parliament and on the 18th February 1642/3 the Commons ordered "That the Plate of the Bishop of Elye shall be melted down forthwith and employed for the Service of the Commonwealth."

In 1646 all bishoprics in the country were suppressed and the Palace at Downham came into the hands of sequestrators. It was alleged by the Royalists that these men took care to turn the sequestration to their own advantage. At an inquisition conducted at Cambridge in the Red Lion inn twenty years later it was sworn by witnesses that there was taken out of the Bishop's park and house at Downham £700 in value and not more than £140 accounted for; that the sequestrators sold the goods distrained upon to each other.

In a letter written to the Guildhall Committee in London on the 16th December 1648 the two Ely sequestrators Luke Voyce the draper and Richard Ponsonby, servant to Cromwell, write of the difficulties they encountered in their task. "Sure we are", they write, "our service has been as dangerous to ourselves as any in the kingdome, in regard to the opposition we have found and in the detestation of the opposite party; besides the extreme hazard of our persons & estates in case the wheel should turn, by seizing and sequestering mens goods, which danger is greater than that of any solicitor; yea than of any soldier that hath fought against the other party."

When at the Restoration of the Monarchy the Bishop was finally released from his imprisonment the Downham estate was in the hands of a certain Arthur Young. "All that capital messuage or mansion house in Downham called 'Le Place', with dovehouse, dwelling house, courts, yards, gardens, orchards, mills & stables. And all that park enclosed by fences & ditches, containing two hundred & ninety one acres. And all those lands called Lowgrounds of meadow and pasture with the part adjoining called 'le ffriths'." All of this estate had been leased to "James Best of Downeham" and the Bishop brought an action for its recovery. The buildings had suffered some demolition, for the prosecution lists goods and chattels of which the Bishop had been robbed. "A thousand laths valued ten pounds; twenty pieces of timber, ten pounds; three boxes of glass, seven pounds; twenty iron bars, eighty shillings; eight pieces of wainscot, eight pounds; ten cartloads of timber, ten pounds and ten of freestone, twenty pounds."

The Downham Palace, once renowned as Bishop Alcock's "praty palace in ye fenne", was never restored, and although much of the fabric still exists, now serving as farm buildings, the only part which remains to testify to the splendour of Alcock's architecture is the chapel with its magnificent doorway virtually intact.

It is plain that the palace had suffered desecration shortly after Bishop Wren's arrest, for when William Balam, who occupied the farm, died in 1684 his son wrote to Bishop Turner, who had just been advanced to the bishopric, and begged to be allowed to take on the tenancy, since he and his brother had a considerable amount of money invested in growing crops and stocks of cattle. His letter continues "My Lord, there is yet a higher reason why I would continew it which is as well your interest of religion as my own, for I can make all the advantage proposed by letting the lands apart from the mansion house, the only useful part of which is in truth a consecrated chappel. Our Act Books are full of Ordinations frequently there celebrated, and it has often wounded my thoughts to see the milk bowles stand there where formerly ye Altar did; a higher prophanation can hardly bee then this. The Tower will suffice for two or three lodging rooms."

Downham Palace Chapel Door.   Photo Willis Grant

In spite of William Balam's declared intention of "forming it into as hansome a seat for a private Gentleman as any in this country" Bishop Turner declined to extend the lease in his favour.

Bishop Wren never returned to his palace at Downham, nor indeed to that at Ely, which even before the "troubles" had been allowed to fall into decay to such an extent that the Chantry on the Green could be noted as "standing right against the Gate of the Bishop's demolisht Palace". He certainly paid a visit to the city in the spring of 1662 and the Dean & Chapter made a payment of £1 "to Mr. Wibrow by Mr. Dean's appointment for his paines in attending the coming of my Lord of Ely to Ely." But when he wrote to the Ely Justices in 1665 banning the St. Awdry's and St. Luke's fairs on account of the plague Bishop Wren dated his letter "Oct. 5th 1665 From my house at Wilburton". He died two years later at the age of 82 and was buried in the chapel of Pembroke College at Cambridge.

Downham Palace. Photo Willis Grant

Proposed demolition.

On the 30th April 1649 Parliament made an order for the lands of Deans & Chapters to be taken over and sold. There had even been proposals to demolish the Cathedral. Earlier in the year, on March 3rd, the Commons ordered:-

"That it be referred to the Committee for sick and wounded soldiers to consider of & examine the structure of the Cathedral Church in the Isle of Ely in relation to the ruinous condition of the same; and what other churches there are in the same place for the people to meet together in, for the hearing of the Word of God, and communicating in the Ordinances of God, and to bring in an Ordinance as they shall find the business, for making sale of the materials of the said Cathedral, that out of the proceed thereof provision may be made for the relief of sick & maimed soldiers, widows &' orphans."

There is no doubt that the Cathedral was, and had been for many years in a state of disrepair, but fortunately not so structurally unsound as to warrant its demolition.

Of the thirteen Commissioners appointed to dispose of the Dean & Chapter properties John Hand and William Austen had served with Cromwell as Governors of Parson's Charity. William Tucke, William Piggot, Richard & Thomas Gotobed, Henry Tingey, John Taylor and Gabriell Leggett had been signatories to the petitions of 1642. Robert Mayes was a prominent member of Holy Trinity and had been Churchwarden and Treasurer of Parson's Charity. Neither William Frost nor Daneill Willson was capable of signing his name; they could only make their marks.

Francis Dicken appears to have come to Ely in the service of Richard Stane, Dr. of Phisick, who was one of the Magistrates for the Isle and who resided in the Chantry on the Green. Writing of the Chantry after his release from prison Bishop Wren remarked "that in Oliver's time it was seized upon by a special favourite of his and now goes for an inheritance". It had in fact passed out of the possession of the church many years earlier — at the Reformation in the sixteenth century.

Dr. Stane was certainly a leading figure in the Parliamentary cause in Ely throughout the Commonwealth period and had little regard for Royalist sympathisers. When in April 1650 Thomas Harrison of Ely was charged with pilfering a pair of shoes belonging to Parliamentary Captain Fowler of Chettisham, for swearing several oaths and for being drunk, he was brought before Dr. Stane. Harrison proved contumacious of authority, and cried "The divell in hell take you and your captain." He was committed to the house of correction "not to be released but by ye Justice of the Peace and until he payes five shillings for oathes, and for being druncke to sitt three houres in the stockes".

There is an air of detachment about the Commissioners' survey of the ancient buildings in the College. With little regard for the architectural worth of the monastic buildings proposals were made for the demolition of many of them with an insensitivity which fully illustrates the severely practical approach of the commissioners to their task. Many of the buildings had of course long since been converted into residences for members of the Cathedral establishment, although some of the prebendal dignitaries had apparently small appreciation of the privilege which was theirs. The commissioners now coldly calculated the value of the building materials which would be available on demolition, and had their proposals been followed much of the domestic architecture for which Ely is justly renowned would have been lost. Fortunately it proved that the cost of demolition would have been so great that the proposals were abandoned as unrealistic.

What happened within the Cathedral is a matter for conjecture, but there was evidently no attempt to demolish any considerable part of the church. The picture presented to us is one rather of neglect and decay than of deliberate destruction. The damage which the fabric had sustained by reason of the negligence of the early years of the century was no doubt accentuated by the long period of disuse which followed the suppression of the Cathedral services, and travellers' accounts of what they found here some years after the Restoration of the Monarchy make very depressing reading.

Depredations.
It may be that some of the fabric was subjected to the depredations of

acquisitive and unscrupulous men. The commissioners in 1649 noted that "Jo: Dickings, Captain Stane his servant hath some lead which came off the Cloysters which Cobb's sonne left when he was taken in the cutting of them; Goodman Clare hath more." Edward Cobb was son of Christopher, the hell-fire preacher, and was a source of great sorrow to his father. In one of his sermons the preacher deplores the degenerate times in which he finds himself. "Children," he says, "children shall rise up against their parents to put them to death. And how hath this proved true in my own child coming as the main witness against me? He was not ashamed to witness falsely against me, and say to my face 'He would take a hundred oaths if he might but ensnare me."

The costly glass and lead from windows and roofs was particularly vulnerable. Whether or not the priceless mediaeval stained glass had been destroyed by the orders of Bishop Goodrich or whether some had survived until the Commonwealth period it is clear that as late as the year 1659 a vast quantity of glass and lead was being stored in the "workhouse" which occupied the whole of the then very dilapidated south transept at the west end, later to be restored and dedicated as the chapel of St. Catherine. Here in February 1660 John Dunch the plumber "found one Nicholas Freeman a putting up glass lead in a sack and likewise glass." Thomas Evans deposed that "to his knowledge there was a great quantitie of lead and glass in the Glass house belonging to ye Cathedral Church"· and he saw Freeman "take away both lead and glass out of ye said Glass house to a very great quantity, and that all ye glass and lead is gone out of ye said house and that there is none left".

Evans stated further that William Tanner and William Gotobed hired him to take lead out of the church and "would have had him pulle one gutter of lead that layd so ferme that it might have lasted this sixtie yeares. He did immediately forsake the worke and would not assist them, but went away & left divers persons a taking lead of ye said Church".

It is clear that these operations were conducted by the direction of the sequestrators, for Nicholas Freeman stated in his defence that Doctor Stane, William Tanner and William Gotobed sold to him "as much lead as he paid eight pownds which was the lead that was taken of the Cathedral & wayed ten hundred & thre quarters, which eight pownds was paid into the hands of William Tanner".

William Gotobed had been "lately a trooper" in the Parliament army.

What is equally clear is that these prosecutions were the result of the swing of public opinion in the direction of the Monarchy. Cromwell had died not quite· twelve months earlier and negotiations were already afoot to restore Charles to the throne.

Charles II landed at Dover on May 25th 1660, to the pealing of bells from churches throughout the country; the ringers of St. Mary's in Ely received a payment of 6s 8d for their services on the occasion. But a fortnight earlier, on the twelfth of the month, Parson's Charity had expended "by the consent of the ffeoffees at the most joyful & happy Proclamation of our Most Gracious Sovereigne Charles the Second upon the xij of May 1660 the sume of £10.8s.10d."

Restoration & recovery.

Richard Love, Master of Corpus, was appointed Dean of Ely on 6th September 1660 and immediately took steps to deal with the situation in which he found himself. Although Parliament declared in November that the sales of church lands made during the Commonwealth were void, the onus of proving title was placed on the newly restored Deans & Chapters, and Dean Love during the short period of his office at Ely (he died in 1661) was assiduous in his search among the documents at the Assize Office in London for the title deeds of the capitular properties. In not all cases was he successful and some of the lands and properties which had been sold were lost to the church forever.

It is from the proceedings which were instigated in the following year that we learn of the fate of the Cathedral furnishings. Dean Stubbs, writing in the late 19th century, entertained "the confident belief that the pre-Reformation organ was not removed or injured by the Puritan soldiers who at Ely were under the personal command of Cromwell. Silenced, no doubt, it was, and silent it continued to be, together with the anthems which it had accompanied, for many dreary years." Stubbs was apparently unaware that the organ had in fact been removed by the sequestrators. At the Assize held at Wisbech on the 3rd October 1660 Edward Cobb of Ely St. Mary's was presented for "pulling downe & careing away the Organs out of the Cathedrall Church of Ely" and confessed to the truth of the charge.

Luke Voyce the elder, of Ely Trinity, admitted "taking away the Church Plate & Vestments" as did also Joseph Cole of Littleport and James Whinnell of Wisbech. Whinnell, who from 1632 to 1680 was Town Bailiffe of Wisbech, confessed to being concerned with Luke Voyce and Joseph Cole in "pulling downe & taking away the Cloth of Arras at the East end of the quier" and also "the Comunion Carpett & Pulpitt Cloth with the Cushion belonging to the said Cathedrall."

In September 1662 an action was brought against Whinnell and Cole for the recovery of the property of the Dean & Chapter "whom they did cunningly & deceitfully cheat & defraud" and evidence was given that there was found in Whinnell's possession at March on the 21st of August 1659:-

> three silver plates gilded, to the value of fifteen pounds
> two silver cupps, to the value of fifteen pounds,
> two silver mazes, to the value of twelve pounds,
> one Bason & Ewer of silver, to the value of twelve pounds
> and
>> the hangings of the Altar, of velvet embroidered with
>> gold, containing twenty yards, to the value of one
>> hundred pounds.

It was claimed that although the Dean & Chapter often made requests for these goods to be returned the miscreants "did not deliver them up, but converted and disposed of them to their own use".

Whinnell freely admitted that the articles were in his possession, but claimed that they had been acquired by him "in the way of trade"; he had obviously purchased them from the sequestrators. In the event it would seem that the gold-embroidered altar hangings had to be replaced by something less magnificent, for on the 17th of July 1662 the Dean & Chapter paid "To Mr. Daye for his worke upon the Damask Cloath &c for the Alter & Quier £6.5.0d, and expended 4s.0d on "a Messenger to Cambridge about ye Hangings of the Alter".

The organ too had been irretrievably lost and had to be replaced. During the Autumn of 1661 £65 was "Expended for the Orgaine bought for the use of the Quier & for bringing of it down to Ely".

And the vexed question of sermons in the parish churches, which aroused so much feeling in 1642, was resolved in no uncertain manner. On the 27th October 1662 the Chapter agreed "That warning shall be given to the two parishes to come to Sermon at the Cathedrall at our Lady day next. In the meantime to provide their Seats".